Helion & Company Limited
Unit 8 Amherst Business Centre
Budbrooke Road
Warwick
CV34 5WE
England
Tel. 01926 499 619
Email: info@helion.co.uk
Website: www.helion.co.uk
Twitter: @helionbooks
Visit our blog http://blog.helion.co.uk/

Designed & typeset by Farr out Publications, Wokingham, Berkshire
Cover design by Paul Hewitt, Battlefield Design (www.battlefield-design.co.uk)

ISBN 978-1-912866-23-1

British Library Cataloguing-in-Publication Data
A catalogue record for this book is available from the British Library

We always welcome receiving book proposals from prospective authors.

CONTENTS

Note: In order to simplify the use of this book, all names, locations and geographic designations are as provided in *The Times World Atlas*, or other traditional accepted major sources of reference, as of the time of described events. For example, the modern-day Republic of Namibia is usually cited as South West Africa because that designation of this territory remained in use in the English language while it was under South African administration, from 1915 until 1990 - despite the decision of the United Nations General Assembly from 1968, which changed its designation into Namibia.

ABBREVIATIONS

COIN	counter-insurgency
COMIRA	Conselho Militar para a Resistência de Angola (Military Council of Angolan Resistance; faction of the FNLA)
DRC	Democratic Republic of the Congo (Congo-Kinshasa, also Zaire)
DTA	Divisão dos Transportes Aéreos (Division of Air Transports, 1938-1973)
ELNA	Exército de Libertação Nacional de Angola (Angola National Liberation Army), FNLA armed wing
EPLA	Exército Popular de Libertação de Angola (Popular Army for the Liberation of Angola)
FALA	Forças Armadas de Libertação de Angola (Angola Liberation Armed Forces; armed wing of UNITA)
FAP	Força Aérea Portuguesa (Portuguese Air Force)
FNLA	Frente Nacional de Libertação de Angola (Angola National Liberation Front)
FRA	Frente de Resistência Angolana (Angolan Resistance Front)
MPLA	Movimento Popular de Libertacao de Angola (People's Movement for the Liberation of Angola)
PIDE	Policia Internacional e de Defesa do Estado (International and State Defence Police)
RPG	rocket-propelled grenade (launcher)
RIM	motorised infantry regiment (official FAR terminology)
SAAF	South African Air Force
SADF	South African Defence Forces
SWA	South West Africa (present day Namibia)
SWAPO	South West African People's Organisation (insurgency in the former South West Africa)
TAAG	Transportes Aéreos Angolanos (Angolan Air Transport, later TAAG, Angola Airlines)
UNITA	União Nacional para a Independência Total de Angola (National Union for the Total Independence of Angola)
Unimog	UNIversal-MOtor-Gerät (range of multi-purpose, all-drive trucks manufactured by Daimler and sold under Mercedes Benz)
UPA	Uniao das Populações de Angola (Angola's People's Union)
USA	United States of America
USSR	Union of Soviet Socialist Republics (or Soviet Union)

ACKNOWLEDGEMENTS

This book would not have been possible without the generous help of Lieutenant Colonel (Cavalry) Miguel Freire, who has made researching the dragoons in Angola a personal interest and who generously shared his findings. He spent many hours with me providing context to his research, for which I am most grateful.

I am likewise indebted to my good friend Colonel (Cavalry) Paulo Manuel Madeira de Athayde Banazol, who offered his personal support and took an active interest in the project through the arrangement of contacts that facilitated my research. For his efforts, I am most grateful.

Additionally, this is a story that could not have been told without the assistance and interest of the many veterans of Africa, particularly a number of cavalry officers who shared their photographs for this book: Major General João Gilberto de Mascarenhas de Sousa Soares da Mota, Colonel Fernando Luís Franco da Silva Ataíde, Colonel Vasco Luís Pereira Esteves Ramires, Colonel António Vital Fernandes Faia, Colonel Manuel Urbano Moreira Dias, and Colonel Manuel Maria Pinheiro da Neves Veloso.

Importantly, I owe much to the wisdom and patience of Duncan Rogers, my publisher, who has seen me through the release now of eight books and to Tom Cooper, who spent many hours editing this book.

Finally, I owe a particular debt to my wife Anne, who lived patiently with the domestic chaos of this work.

INTRODUCTION

Between 1961 and 1974, Portugal faced the extremely ambitious task of conducting three simultaneous counterinsurgency campaigns in Guiné, Angola, and Mozambique. It was at the time neither a wealthy nor a well-developed country. In fact, it was the least wealthy Western European nation by most standards of economic measure. Thus, for Portugal in 1961 to have mobilized an armed force, transported it many thousands of miles to its African colonies, established a sophisticated logistic infrastructure to support it, equipped it with special weapons and matériel, and trained it for a very specialized type of warfare was a remarkable achievement. It is made even more noteworthy by the fact that these tasks were accomplished without any previous experience, doctrine, or demonstrated competence in the field of either power projection or counterinsurgency warfare, and thus without the benefit of any instructors who were competent in these specialties. To put this last statement in perspective, other than periodic pacification efforts, Portugal had not fired a shot in anger in Africa since World War One, when Germany invaded northern Mozambique and southern Angola.

The Portuguese defence establishment was quite familiar with the principles of counterinsurgency, was aware that its troops were not going to fight a classic conventional war, and understood that forces had to be modified and adapted to the job at hand. There was substantial concern throughout the armed forces in undertaking what would be a wholesale and radical change in force structure and training, as it would affect all aspects of traditional tactics, techniques, and procedures. It would very much disturb the status quo and thus professional career paths. Nevertheless, Portugal proceeded to adapt its forces to a new way of war and created a force uniquely tailored to fight in this new struggle. It changed its forces to fit the war rather than trying to fight a war with the wrong forces.

One of the most noteworthy of these developments was the use of specially tailored forces to hunt the insurgents. Because of the vastness and the terrain and extreme variation in the battlefield, there was specialisation within these forces. The reintroduction of horse cavalry was one of the most unique and relied on an old solution to an old problem. Employed in the expansive savannas of eastern Angola and later in the highlands of Mozambique between 1966 and 1974, these units were used to patrol vast and difficult terrain that was impossible for wheeled vehicles and helicopters, the former being unable to negotiate the terrain and the latter flying over the population that it needed to protect. In the following pages we will explore just how a reinvigorated horse cavalry within the Portuguese Army brought security to these difficult areas and examine their organisation, employment, and effectiveness in doing so.

1
WHY HORSE CAVALRY?

For Portugal in the twentieth century, the horse did not fade from combat into the ceremonial background, as it did in most other modern militaries. In fact, in Africa between 1966 and 1974, it proved the solution to mobility in areas that, while not enormously difficult, still in their own way presented severe challenges in terrain and provided insurgents with a fertile medium for operations. It was in these areas of large savanna plains in central Angola and in the highlands of Mozambique that were too expansive to patrol on foot, particularly with Portuguese manpower limitations, and unsuited for wheeled vehicles with the tall elephant grass and frequent rivers, that the horse proved its value. While the helicopter was considered ideal, there were too few of them, and their unique requirements were often needed more imperatively elsewhere. The helicopter also had the disadvantage in its operational tendency to fly over the populations of these areas where communication with the people, securing their loyalty, and gathering intelligence were vital.

The partial solution to the shape of a proper force was found in history. Horse cavalry had first been used in Angola in 1571 and had participated in the early battles of Canbambe (1583) and of Rio Lucala (1590).[1] At Canbambe, for instance, it was said that one man mounted was equal to near a hundred enemy on foot.[2] These and subsequent experiences through the 1915 actions in the south of Angola formed a reservoir of knowledge that led to the horse as a solution to mobility and policing in modern counterinsurgency and to our story about the modern dragoons in austral Africa.

Historical Perspective

Love of the horse in Portugal dates to prehistoric times and to what is now the Alentejo, where the remains of the Sorraia breed have been discovered and dated from 25,000 BC. Prehistoric cave paintings dated between 17,000 and 13,000 BC in Santiago de Escoural reinforce the importance of the horse in early western Iberia.[3] Remains of riding tack and weapons further show that in the Neolithic era (4500–2000 BC) horses were being used for combat in southern Portugal, a time when domesticated horses were still unknown in other parts of the world, let alone being ridden and used in combat.[4] This is remarkable, as battle horses had to be very nimble and anticipate the needed moves in a fight, such as turning and stopping, for rider and horse to survive and prevail – skills that required sophisticated training to execute effectively. These were light horsemen who were each equipped with a helmet and perhaps, later, a coat of mail, a light shield (adarga), a short lethal sword (falcata), and a lance.[5] When engaged in combat, the rider with his fellow horsemen would circle their opponents, hovering beyond their reach and looking for an opening to enable a lightning and deadly strike.[6] This swarming harassment would continue until the enemy, exhausted, gave ground or broke his formation in disorder and provided the opportunity to execute a critical charge and together with infantry enter a melee.[7] The training and dexterity of the horse were vital to this art of fighting.

When the Romans during their three Punic Wars with Carthage (264–146 BC) established a presence in Western Iberia, then known as Lusitania, they quickly gained respect for the horsemanship of the locals. These Lusitanians and their horse-mounted style of warfare were so admired by the Romans that they adopted it. It was superior in mobility and manoeuvrability to anything they had seen. This led to the local establishment of Lusitanian horse breeding estates for Roman cavalry. The collapse of Roman rule in 409 AD provided a power vacuum and consequent invasion by the Visigoths, who ruled until the Moors of the Umayyad Caliphate assaulted Gibraltar in 711 and completed their conquest of most of the Iberian Peninsula shortly thereafter. The Moors occupied the old Roman province of Lusitania (the central and southern regions of present-day Portugal), while Gallaecia (the northern region of present-day Portugal) remained unsubdued. Their occupation lasted some four centuries.

Toward the end of the eleventh century, Alfonso VI, King of Castile and León, with the help of many French knights, began the successful reconquest of New Castile, an area in the northwest of the Peninsula and adjacent to Castile and León. Among the knights were two princes, Henri of Burgundy and his cousin Raymond of

Map of the Iberian Peninsula in 200 BC showing the location of Lusitania and Gallaecia. (Map by the author)

Map of the Iberian Peninsula in 12th Century showing the location of the Kingdoms of León and Navarre and the area of Portucalense. (Map by the author)

Burgundy. After the Moors were driven from New Castile, Alfonso offered his two daughters to the princes in marriage. Urraca, heir to the throne, married Raymond. Teresa, whose dowry was a distant country beyond the Serra de Montesinho, called Portucalense, and at the time occupied by the Moors, married Henri in 1095, making him Count of Portugal. A son was born to them in 1109 and named Afonso Henriques. His father died in 1112, and his mother became regent pending her son's coming of age. However, in 1128 he revolted against her abuse of the regent authority and seized power, which included the right to her dowry. He proceeded to raise an army to reclaim Portucalense, and his first successful campaign began at Ourique in 1139. This victory led to his being acclaimed king by his soldiers. Further successes let to the fall of Lisbon in 1147.

During these campaigns, the Portuguese were generally outnumbered on the battlefield and turned to the horse for an advantage. Reminiscent of the earlier style of fighting from horseback, cavalry was used to wear down the enemy, until he was exhausted and vulnerable. Mounted troops would approach the foe, throw their javelins, and then withdraw before beginning another assault. After softening the enemy with a number of these manoeuvres, the horsemen would charge with thrusting spears and then engage in a melee with a long, double-edged sword designed to fight from a horse. The horsemen wore a mail hauberk and carried a kite shield of wood with a leather cover. Body armour was typically leather with iron scales. The helmet was round with a nose protector and a chain mail headpiece protected the neck and shoulders.

During the ensuing centuries cavalry development on the organised and cooler battlefields of central and northern Europe tended toward heavily armoured knights on large chargers, but Portugal — in its experience — found that a rider unencumbered by heavy armour could sit more easily in the saddle and move with greater speed and agility. This observation dictated a move toward light cavalry as the most effective use of resources, and Portuguese light cavalry tactics featured prominently in fifteenth- and sixteenth-century warfare.[8] Training in fighting from horseback and particularly in throwing a spear at speed to achieve significant distance with accuracy was practiced continually. King Duarte (1391–1438) advised Portuguese cavalrymen to be skilled in all styles

King Afonso Henriques (Afonso I) with his kite shield, round helmet with nose guard, and long, double-edged sword. The statue is in Guimarães, a city in old Gallaecia. (Photograph by Gi Pinto)

of riding and fighting from horseback, a capability that would make them superior to the enemy.[9] The lethality of this cavalry relied on several important characteristics that would remain key, even into modern times:

1 the mobility of the horse,
2 the visibility afforded the mounted rider,
3 the intimidating appearance and danger of a charging horse and rider to an enemy on foot,
4 the silent movement of the horse across ground that allowed surprise, and
5 an indomitable cavalry spirit

These were to serve the Portuguese well in the seventeenth century and beyond as they ventured abroad and gained experience and expertise in fighting in varying climes and terrain. It was certainly to give them an advantage in tropical bush warfare, particularly against enemies unused to the heat and disorganisation of African battlefields.[10]

From Wealth To Penury

As Portugal progressed as a nation, it found itself isolated from Europe by both geography and hostile frontiers, and constantly threatened by its immediate neighbour Spain. It was thus forced to seek its fortune at sea. Initial exploration began with the invasion and seizure of Ceuta in 1415 and the subsequent search for the trade source of the merchants on the North African coast, who came from the interior and across the Sahara by caravan to offer their goods, primarily gold. Seizing Ceuta and learning that the source of the gold was the Upper Niger and Senegal Rivers prompted Portugal to consider diverting this trade to its own ships. Gold was in great demand in Western Europe during the last two and a half centuries of the Middle Ages, the period of European history from the fall of the Roman Empire in the fifth century to the fall of Constantinople in 1453, as gold coinage had been adopted by one city, region, or country after another. This had been inspired by the striking of the Florentine gold florin in 1252 and the Venetian gold ducat around 1280.[11] Portugal was at the time one of the few European countries without a gold currency. Trustworthy money invariably ignited trade and cooperation among strangers that fuelled human achievement, and Portugal wanted to be in the vanguard of this advance.

Consequently, exploration proceeded south along the West African littoral with a generally peaceful trade conducted from Portuguese ships, as they sailed down the coast and anchored in suitable roadsteads or estuaries.[12] In 1461 Portugal established its first trading post or factory (*feitoria*) when it built a fort on the island of Arguim in the bay of the same name in what is present-day Mauritania. Here the Portuguese exchanged horses, cloth, brassware, and corn for gold dust, slaves, and ivory.[13] As the Portuguese pushed south along the African coast, rounded the Cape of Good Hope in 1497, and reached India, Arguim became the prototype for a chain of fortified trading centres constructed along the African and Asian coasts as far as the Moluccas, today eastern Indonesia. The Portuguese managed to defeat both the European and Muslim challenges to their new trading enterprise and proceeded to establish a systematic arc of enclaves strategically ringing the Atlantic and Indian Oceans. These bases commanded both the sources of trade as well as the sea routes themselves. As the Portuguese secured their dominance in this area, so profits from their localised trade as well as the Cape route increased accordingly. Great wealth had awaited the European nation that could directly tap the source of African and Eastern goods, and Portugal succeeded in this challenge. The trade became immensely profitable, and wealth poured into Portugal on an unprecedented scale. Portugal reached its height of power and influence during the first half of the sixteenth century. Its decline can be marked from June 1578 and its disastrous North African campaign in which King Sebastião and his army were destroyed in four hours by Moroccan forces near the town of Al-Ksar al-Kebir (Alcácer Quibir in Portuguese).[14] His force had totalled some 15,000 foot and 1,500 horse with 9,000 camp followers. Five hundred vessels had been required to transport it. Eight thousand were killed, 15,000 were taken prisoner and sold into slavery, and perhaps 100 eventually reached the safety of Portugal to tell of the loss. The might of Portugal was wasted with this disaster, and the next year the great Portuguese epic poet and inspirer of nationalistic sentiment, Luís Vaz de Camões, wrote to a friend from his deathbed in Lisbon, "All will see that so dear to me was my country that I was content to die not only in but with it."[15]

While leaving an indelible imprint on the European perspective of the world, the Portuguese had exhausted themselves in the process. They were never able to regain their sixteenth century stature, and from that period until the twentieth century Portugal experienced an irregular path of decline with episodes of partial recovery. As a nation, the Portuguese have historically looked back on this time, which they call *O Século Maravilhoso* (The Marvellous Century), and longed to regain the former height of glory and greatness. Although this first empire was short-lived, it created a permanent nostalgia, a "vibrant chord of imperial grandeur" around which to rally colonial support.[16] In the period between 1497 and 1578 the Portuguese had established a new concept of empire based on a mastery of the ocean routes. Trade, not territory, was the prime objective. With the death of a childless King Sebastão, the Portuguese throne passed to the aged and ailing Cardinal-King Henry, who died in January 1580. Within a few months King Philip of Spain, whose mother was a Portuguese princess, sought to enforce his claim and was

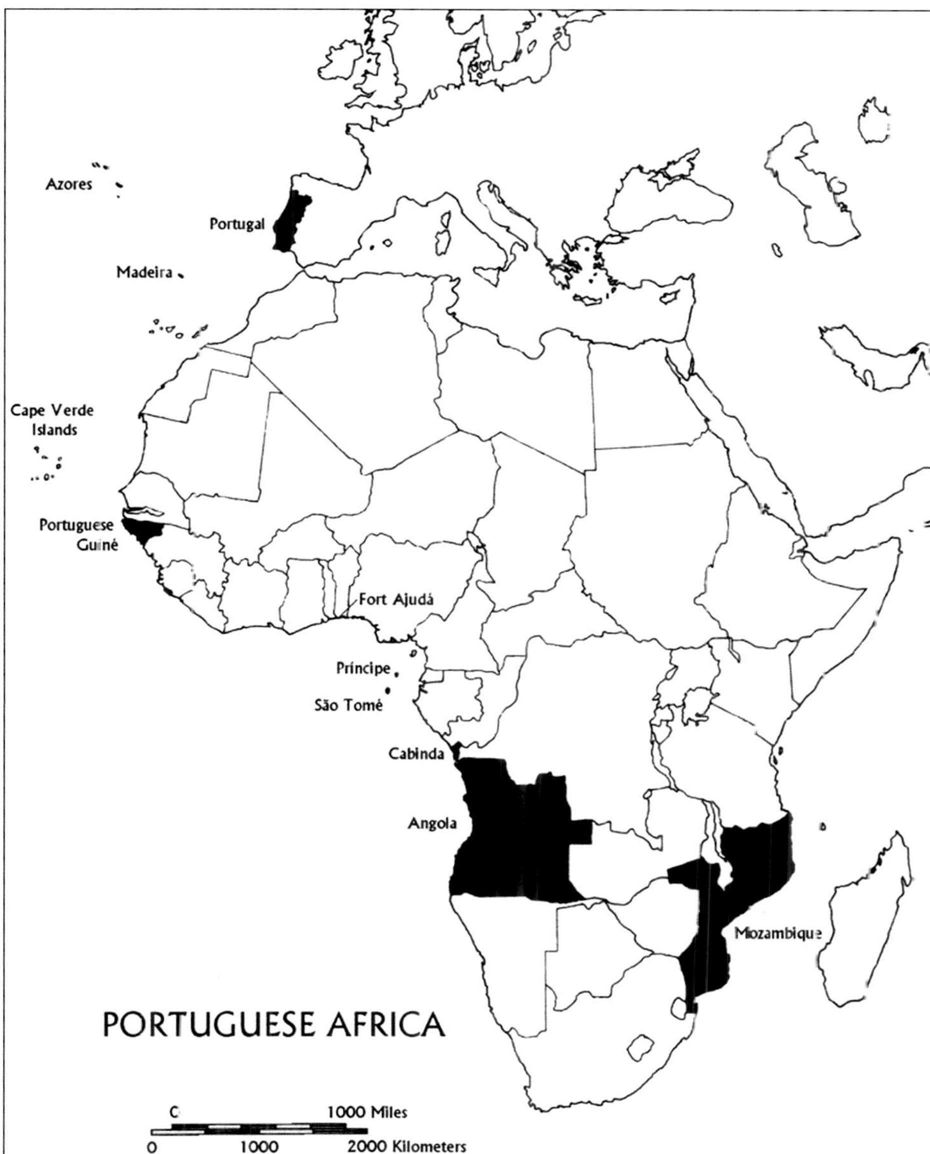

Portuguese Africa. (Map by the author)

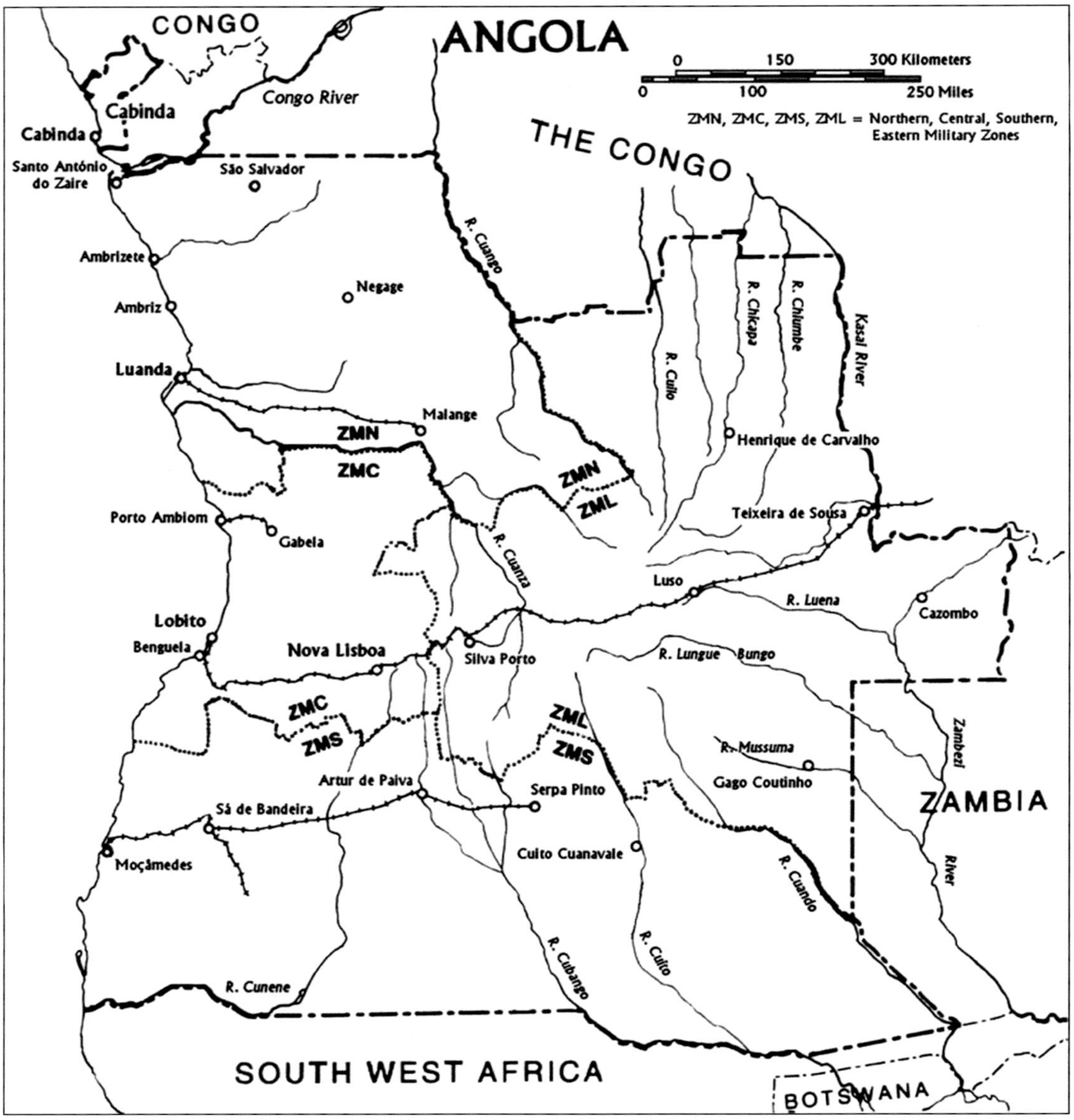

Angola. (Map by the author)

successful in undermining opposition within Portugal. The Crowns of Spain and Portugal were thus united between 1580 and 1640, and Portuguese trade dominance was effectively lost to competitor nations. When Portugal recovered its independence in 1640, it was a wonder that it retrieved so much of its overseas holdings as well, particularly its colonies of Angola, Brazil, and Mozambique. As spices were the single most lucrative commodity of the sixteenth century, so Brazilian sugar replaced them in the seventeenth century. When West Indian sugar production threatened to supplant that of Brazil, gold was discovered there in 1694. In 1728 diamonds were discovered. The revenue from this colonial wealth maintained the continuity of Portuguese prosperity, until Brazil declared its independence in 1822 following the relocation of the king there in 1807, when the French invaded the Iberian Peninsula. It was the memory of Brazil and the wealth that it had provided that generated a twentieth century hope for a similar prosperity from the African colonies. This Brazilian model, in which "Portuguese language and culture were firmly entrenched," became a far more influential guide for the development of Angola and Mozambique than *O Século Maravilhoso*.[17] These two colonies were seen potentially as modern-day Brazils and the prized keys to renewed prosperity and greatness.

Napoleonic Influence

Over the years leading to the Napoleonic Wars, cavalry became expensive relative to musket-armed infantry. Armoured cavalrymen were costly to train and maintain, as it took years to develop a skilled horse and rider and meld them into an effective force. Heavy cavalry was composed of large, strong men mounted on large, strong horses. Such a combination was excellent for its shock effect on the battlefield when organised into a disciplined, cohesive formation in a massive, irresistible charge. Only wealthy nations could afford the enormous and costly amounts of food, equipment, and training needed for such a force. Aside from being expensive, heavy cavalry did not have the stamina to pursue an enemy, to skirmish, or even to escort a convoy well. It was mission-specific with the associated limitations.

Consequently, there evolved a lighter, more agile cavalry that was used in an entirely different way on the battlefield. Its concept was to be the advance eyes and ears of the army, scouting ahead of its route and protecting its flanks. In contrast to its heavier counterpart, light cavalry foraged for the army and was capable of enemy pursuit. Riders were also able to fight on foot, and this capability provided enormous flexibility. The commander who could rapidly move a large body of infantry on horseback, called dragoons, to a critical point in the fight held a great advantage. This was the model that Portugal sought.

The trauma to Portugal of the French invasions between 1807 and 1814 clearly showed the need for a proper armed force and a serious approach to establishing it, as the Portuguese military had experienced a long period of decline under Spanish rule (1580–1640) and had never truly recovered. The initial focus of this effort was the formation of professional infantry and cavalry units; however, this was postponed because of the Liberal Wars fought from 1828 to 1834 between the progressive constitutionalists and the authoritarian absolutists over Portuguese royal succession. Once succession was settled, and Maria II resumed her interrupted reign, work continued. At this time cavalry units tended to be local in both recruitment and training, which meant that there was an appreciable variation in capability from unit to unit. This lack of consistency existed, because there was no central organisation with a reservoir of experienced instructors and standardised training to ensure that the level of skills was both elevated and consistent. There was also a scarcity of horses and fodder that dictated this decentralised approach.

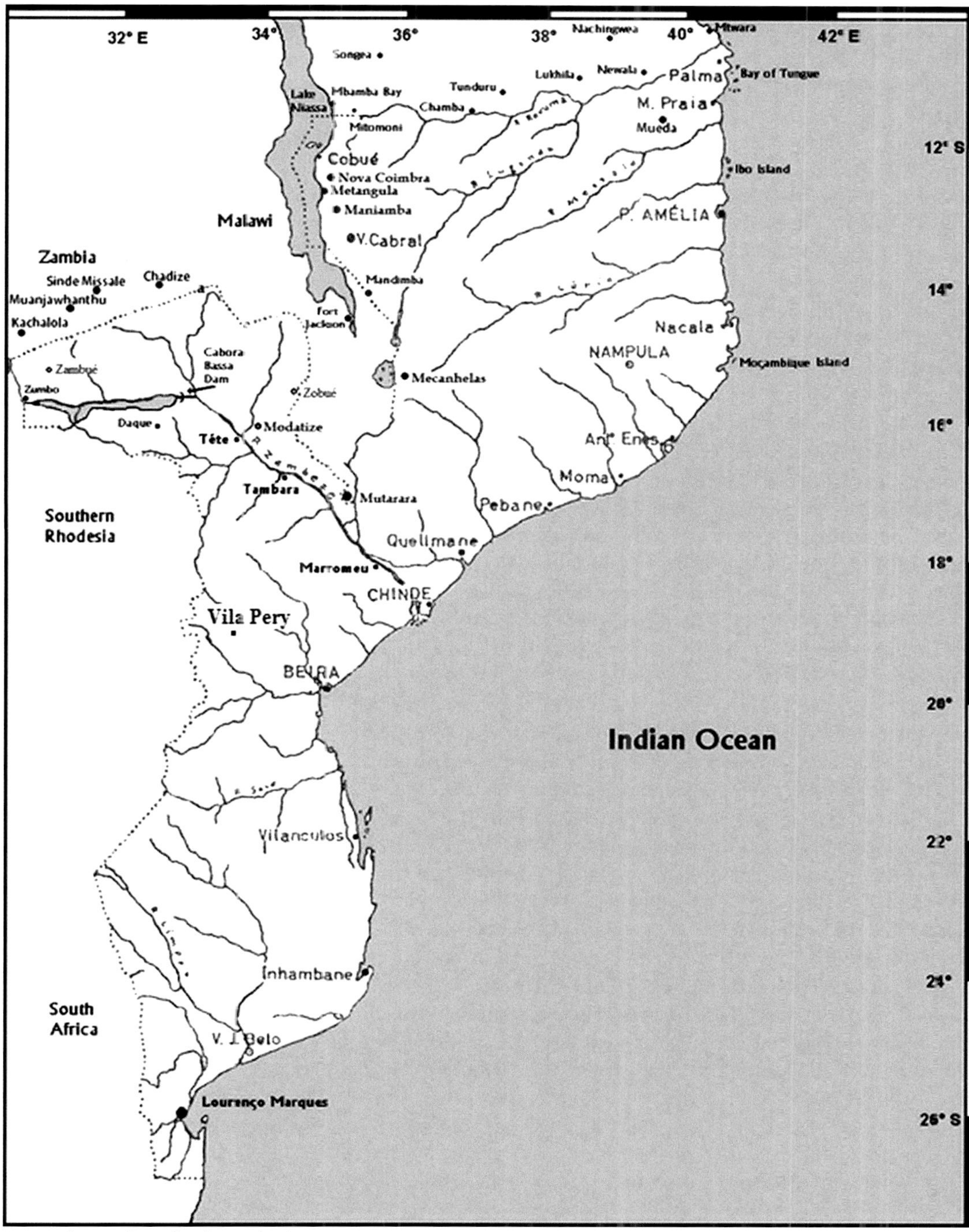

Mozambique. (Map by the author)

A compelling reason for this regionalisation was the practical logistics of feeding a horse. For instance, a 1,000-pound horse required ten pounds of corn and twenty pounds of good forage a day. This translated into a half to a full acre of good grazing land. The topography of Portugal, as well as its poor infrastructure, could not naturally provide this to sustain any sizable centralised cavalry force.[18] Portugal would need to solve this limitation in forming a national cavalry force.

By the late nineteenth century Portugal was in financial straits. In 1870 it suffered an economic crisis in which the government was effectively rendered bankrupt, as it faced enormous arrears on its national debt. Although the crisis appeared temporary, in fact it was a clear notice that the balance between the agricultural world of southern Europe and its industrial north had decisively shifted against Portugal.[19] This strategic reversal and its economic consequences prompted a fresh urgency for Portugal to find new overseas wealth in its undeveloped African territories as a long-term solution to its adversity.

Subsequently during the 1870s, this urgency manifested itself in a push to complete military pacification of its African colonies, as these keys to prosperity were overtly threatened by Germany and Great Britain, both of which wished to expand their neighbouring possessions at the expense of Portugal. This threat, which culminated in what became known as the British Ultimatum of 1890, developed in the last two decades of the nineteenth century, when the industrial economies of northern Europe were expanding dramatically, and there was an urgent need for raw materials to feed this growth. This economic pressure translated into a spontaneous "scramble for Africa," a frantic rush by the more prosperous European powers to establish colonial claims and seek new opportunities amid an increasing European awareness about Africa.

In this fluid environment the Portuguese intention was to join Angola and Mozambique through austral Africa, potentially to form a second Brazil. Portugal had launched expeditions by Alexandre de Serpa Pinto, Hermenegildo Capelo, Roberto Ivens, and Henrique de Carvalho between 1877 and 1885 to explore this claimed territory, and thus from the de facto perspective viewed itself as already in possession of this land. Consequently, following the treaties with Germany and France resulting from the Berlin Conference of 1885 on the ownership of Africa, Portugal published the 'Rose-Coloured Map", which showed Angola and Mozambique united in a coast-to-coast colony. Britain became alarmed at the vigour and direction of Portuguese colonial policy, which seemed so "unprecedented and out of character," and the "unwonted" success of its exploration and military operations, that it feared humiliation at the devious hand of the "despised" Portuguese.[20] At the insistence of the opportunist Cecil Rhodes, Britain took strong exception to Portuguese claims, and in June 1887, Lord Salisbury, the British foreign minister, stated that the British would "not recognise Portuguese sovereignty in territories not occupied with sufficient forces to maintain order."[21] As David Abshire has observed, "To his government it did not matter how many ruined forts, churches, and other relics that the Portuguese could show. It mattered only whether the Portuguese could keep law and order in the areas and control them."[22]

Portugal, nevertheless, proceeded with its colonial expansion plans, and the ardent imperialist Serpa Pinto boldly advanced into a British preserve near Lake Niassa in what is now southern Malawi. As a consequence, on 11 January 1890, Salisbury demanded Portugal's immediate withdrawal from the questioned area and backed the demand with a threat of force in mobilising the British fleet. Portugal withdrew accordingly in great humiliation. This Ultimatum, and its consequences were to make Mozambique a coastal colony with no hinterland and British territory landlocked with no outlet to the sea. Mozambique remained separated from Angola by between 500 and 700 kilometres, and Portugal's ambition for a grand coast-to-coast colony unrealised. Portuguese claims were far superior to those of Britain. When Portugal established what was clearly effective occupation, Salisbury switched tact and condemned the occupation of areas claimed by Britain even when unsupported by any British presence.[23]

After Brazilian independence in 1822, the development of the vast linked colonies of Angola and Mozambique remained the last hope for any substantial renewal of prosperity. If one views the territory that was lost to Britain and its imperial developer Cecil Rhodes from a twenty-first century perspective, it is easy to see that the hinterland wealth of the Rhodesias and portions of the Belgian Congo, when connected to the Atlantic and Indian Ocean outlets of Angola and Mozambique, would have indeed given Portugal a second Brazil. The magnitude of this loss became a Portuguese preoccupation thereafter and was to solidify its national attitude in the absolute sacredness of its remaining territories abroad.

British colonial ambitions in the area reflected those of Rhodes, an inveterate territorial privateer who made even Salisbury concerned about further Portuguese humiliation. The Ultimatum had struck at the roots of the Portuguese monarchy, whose popular support rested in part on the assumption that the Portuguese crown was a magic link to British protective power, a link that dated from the initial Anglo-Portuguese alliance of 13 June 1373.[24] The Ultimatum undermined this concept and increased the unpopularity on the king. It also brought into relief the British view of the Portuguese embodied in the Victorian concept of imperialism in that if Portugal was unable to fulfil its colonising mission, then the "white man's burden" should pass to those more capable.[25] It was often assumed that the disintegration of Portuguese Africa was simply a matter of time and that the British would be its heirs. Such attitudes and assumptions spawned a number of secret agreements, the key one being between Britain and Germany to divide Portuguese possessions should its empire crumble.[26] Portuguese financial weakness played an important part in this development.

Germany, a relatively late arrival in Africa, had at the time a number of widely separated territories. It sought to link them through further acquisitions and thus assure what it viewed as its rightful place in the modern colonial expansion. This linking was to occur in great part through the liquidation of the Portuguese possessions, specifically Britain and Germany would divide them so that Germany would receive southern and northern Angola, and Britain its centre. Northern Mozambique and Timor would also go to Germany, while southern Mozambique would become British. The German government then initiated a policy of pénétration pacifique, in which it began a diplomatic and financial offensive to weaken the Portuguese hand in Africa.[27] Portuguese leadership was aware of this scheming and remained determined to stay in Africa as a national policy. It thus began to take the concept of effective occupation seriously as part of its national strategy, particularly in light of the lesson of the Ultimatum, that the rules applied to the great powers would be different from those applied to Portugal.[28]

As this threat developed, it focused the military, forced its reorganisation, and accelerated the desire to create a dedicated centre of instruction for its principal armed specialities of infantry and cavalry. The first step was the creation in Mafra of the Practical School of Infantry and Cavalry (Escola Prática de Infantaria e Cavalaria) in 1887.[29] From this beginning, Mafra became the principal source of trained personnel for the needed military expansion; however, it soon proved inadequate to support defence requirements of both the metrópole (continental Portugal) and the ultramar (overseas Portugal), as it lacked the necessary space to accommodate the growing training need. Consequently in 1890, the cavalry portion of the Mafra school was closed and a new school opened in Vila Viçosa, the Practical School of Cavalry (Escola Prática de Cavalaria).

At Vila Viçosa there developed two primary types of cavalry units, dragoons and lancers, although this did not preclude other light cavalry units with such duties as scouting, foraging, pursuit, screening, gathering intelligence, skirmishing, and on occasion initiating shock action. Dragoons, essentially mounted infantry, were capable of fighting from horse or on foot. With the mobility of their mounts, dragoons could move rapidly to a decisive point and change the battle equation.

Lancers were armed with a 2.5-metre-long lance that on the march was set into a small cup on the stirrup to support its weight. It was held in place by a sling around the rider's arm. Mastery of the lance required extensive training, practice, and a strong hand, as simply giving lances to poorly trained men did not make them competent lancers, merely "horsemen with sticks."[30] On the other hand a squadron of lancers was a formidable opponent – terrifying in an orderly and thunderous charge with the constant beat of the hooves and the men shouting. The preservation of good order during a charge was difficult yet critical for proper effect. Obstacles on the battlefield, stress, and over-excitement could and did threaten order, so continuous practice was needed to counter anticipated battlefield chaos. The lance itself was an aggressive and dangerous weapon in that its length allowed the cavalryman on first contact to wound or kill an enemy armed with a shorter weapon. The drawback was that once past this initial contact, the lancer became vulnerable. Generally, a charge by lancers was followed by a supporting charge of sabres to handle the ensuing melee and protect the now vulnerable lancers.[31]

For twelve years Portuguese cavalry flourished there, and it was from this institution that pacification expeditions to Angola and Mozambique were launched. Major Joaquim Augusto Mouzinho de Albuquerque was the singularly most famous figure associated with the school during this period, and his contribution to the pacification and governance of Mozambique remains a remarkable feat. While cavalry on the European battlefields to come would cease to be an effective force in the face of massed machinegun fire, it would be important in pacifying Portuguese Africa, and thus horse-mounted cavalry continued to play an important role in Portuguese military planning.

As Mouzinho was to become the unequalled example of the colonial soldier in this epoch of Portuguese renewal and expansion in Africa, it is instructive to trace his development. Born in 1855 in Batalha, Mouzinho became a volunteer recruit in Cavalry Regiment No. 4 in November 1871 at age sixteen. In 1876 he completed the cavalry course at the Army School and was commissioned as a second lieutenant (alferes). From this point onward, his life was the army.

Mouzinho was a charismatic figure with a particular personal

From the azulejo panel representing Major Augusto Mouzinho de Albuquerque installed on the parade at the Practical School of Cavalry. (Practical School of Cavalry)

style. He was thin, tall, and athletic with an erect military carriage. He was a man of action, a characteristic that stood out in a society of "anchovies and sad faces."[32] In contrast to many military officers of his generation, Mouzinho attended Coimbra University between 1879 and 1882 and studied philosophy and mathematics. While he did not receive a degree, he applied himself and acquired a comprehensive understanding of modern Portuguese literature and the skill to write well. He was a military instructor in Lisbon between 1884 and 1886 and took an assignment in Portuguese India between 1886 and 1890, where he studied English, Dutch, and French colonial literature. His contact with English colonial administrators decisively influenced his later work in Mozambique, and he was considered a specialist on the problems of austral Africa.[33]

Mouzinho was promoted to captain at the conclusion of his service in India and next assigned as governor of the district of Lourenço Marques in October 1890, nine months after the Ultimatum. In this billet he experienced first-hand the inertia and inefficiency of the colonial bureaucracies in both the ultramar and the metrópole, and proceeded to govern his district in the style of colonial Britain that he so admired: pragmatism, efficiency, decentralisation of power and control, and attention to local needs over preconceptions or the interests of the metrópole.[34] This approach led to conflict with the governor-general, and Mouzinho returned to Portugal in 1892. There was, however, soon to be another opportunity in Mozambique.

Table 1: List of City/Town/Locality Name Changes in Angola, 1960-today	
Colonial Name	**New Name**
Amboim	Gabela
Benguella	Benguela
Carmona	Uige
Gago Coutinho	Lumbala
Henrique de Carvalho	Saurimo
Luso	Luena
Nova Lisboa	Huambo
Mocamedes	Namibe
Novo Redondo	Sumbe
N'Zeto	Ambrizete
Porto Amboim	Gunza
Pereira de Eça	Ongiva
Porto Alexandre	Tombwe/Tombua
Roçades	Xangongo
Vila Robert Williams	Caála
Sá de Bandeira	Lubango
Salazar	N'Dalatando
Santa Comba/Cela	Waku-Kungo
Santo Antonio de Zaire	Soyo
Sao Salvador	M'banza-Kongo
Serpa Pinto	Menongue
Silva Porto	Kuito
Teixeira da Silva	Bailundo/Bailunda
Teixeira de Sousa	Luau
Xamindele	Toto
Vila Luso	Luena
Vila Salazar	N'dalatando

Mozambique 1895–1896

Portuguese pacification of Mozambique required some 160 military actions involving 16,401 regular troops and 57,983 auxiliaries between 1854 and 1916, and these figures do not include the German invasion and the Portuguese actions associated with it during the 1915–1918 period.[35] Among the most famous and noteworthy of these was the 1895 battle at the settlement of Coolela located in the district of Gaza just to the north of Lourenço Marques, today Maputo. Lourenço Marques was at the time a small town and seaport that had grown around the Fortaleza de Nossa Senhora da Conceição, which had been built in 1781 to secure Portuguese claims against those of other European powers. The town that grew around the fort starting about 1850 was named for Vasco da Gama's navigator, Lourenço Marques. In 1877 it was elevated to city status and in 1898 it became the capital of the colony. The capital at the time of the battle was still located on Moçambique Island in the extreme north of the colony.

The south of Mozambique was threatened by the rise of the local King Gungunhana of Gaza. He attempted to frustrate Portuguese authority and asked the British for protection, which was refused. He then sought contact with other European governments, hoping to gain time in which to build the strength of his forces, but these

Mouzinho de Albuquerque receiving the surrender of Gungunhana at Chaimite immortalised in the bronze panel by Leopoldo de Almeida now located in the museum of military history in Fortaleza da Nossa Senhora da Conceição, Maputo. (Photograph by Diogo Alves)

contacts were counterproductive and cost him the loyalty of many of his people. In 1890 he signed an agreement with the British South Africa Company of Cecil Rhodes, but the British government, fearful of further diplomatic repercussions with Portugal following the Ultimatum, disallowed it. Still Gungunhana and his restive people resisted Portuguese rule.

Consequently, Portugal organised a special expedition to address this threat, and it arrived in Lourenço Marques in April 1895. Mouzinho, now a major, had taken command of Squadron of Lancers No. 2 in Lourenço Marques the previous year, and he and his unit were assigned to this expedition. Progress of the campaign was slow during the initial period April to December, and its advance was frustrated by a combination of tropical conditions, poor communications, and inadequate transport. Under these circumstances a military force could hardly advance rapidly into the heart of the bush that was the Gaza district.[36] Compounding these frictional influences, Colonel Eduardo Galhardo, commander of the expeditionary force, had no experience fighting in Africa, and his excessive caution translated into a very slow and well-advertised advance. All of this annoyed the impatient Mouzinho to no end.

Armed only with a sword and revolver, Mouzinho led his cavalry in many courageous scouting missions into the African interior in the initial months of the campaign. From the beginning, his audacity and bravery earned him the admiration of his countrymen. Sadly, cavalry was not the decisive force in the campaign. It was plainly the machinegun, which proved itself against the masses of African warriors who fought for Gungunhana. The decisive battle occurred on 7 November 1895 at Cooela, where some 12,000 Ngonis with 3,000 rifles were defeated by 577 Portuguese officers and men and about 500 indigenous auxiliaries. The casualties were telling. Some 305 Ngonis were killed and between 600 and 900 wounded. The Portuguese suffered five killed and twenty-seven wounded.[37] As to Mouzinho, his unit lost many horses at Coolela but persisted in its attack on the African lines heedless of the risks.

The lopsided victory broke the authority of Gungunhana over his followers, and he fled northward to the small settlement of Chaimite on the bank of the Limpopo River, where he was among his people. Meanwhile, Lisbon recalled the expeditionary force, as it was the rainy season, and further operations could not be conducted until the late spring. Still Gungunhana remained in hiding, and his location a mystery. On 10 December, Mouzinho, the "hero of Coolela," was appointed military governor of Gaza, and on 12 December he learned the location of Gungunhana at Chaimite through sound intelligence work. In typical bold style, Mouzinho in a courageous move marched with a small group to Chaimite, where Gungunhana surrendered peacefully.[38]

When word reached Lisbon of Mouzinho's success, he became a "hero of Africa" and returned to Lisbon for feting. In a period of "colonial pessimism" and one in which there had been no heroes, Portugal now had one, and Mouzinho's name was on everyone's lips.[39] As to Gungunhana, he was brought to Lisbon with his family, where he stayed briefly before being exiled in June 1896 to the island of Terceira in the Azores. Here he was baptised in the Cathedral of Angra and changed his name to Reinaldo Frederico Gungunhana. He and his family adopted Western ways and became fully assimilated. He died in 1906 and today his descendants live in Angra.

Following Mouzinho's highly public success, he was appointed governor-general of Mozambique in March 1896 and returned to the colony to assume his duties on 21 May. During the ensuing months, he led a successful pacification campaign and participated in the battles of Naguema (3 March), Mocutumudo (6 March) and Macantene (21 July). In this last engagement the governor-general himself together with his chief-of-staff Captain Aires de Ornelas e

Mouzinho de Albuquerque leading the cavalry charge at Macantene immortalised in the bronze panel by Simões de Almeida now located in the museum of military history in Fortaleza da Nossa Senhora da Conceição, Maputo. (Photograph by Diogo Alves)

Vasconcelos, a fellow cavalryman, organised a pacification column to secure the area north of Lourenço Marques to the Limpopo River. They had the necessary means with some four hundred officers and soldiers that included forty-nine cavalrymen.[40] The march for the cavalry was a long, beautiful, and uninterrupted ride that covered two hundred kilometres in thirty-six hours. The remainder of the force came by boat as far as Chai-Chai on the Limpopo River, where it disembarked and joined the cavalry squadron.[41] The force then moved along the length of the Limpopo until Chibuto, where it arrived on 15 July. The march was remarkable in that it was unchallenged, and indeed, no one had even worried the force. The prestige of Mouzinho was such that on the next day about twenty local chiefs came to pay their respects. Mouzinho's wife and two nuns also joined the force to care for the anticipated casualties.[42]

After Chibuto, events evolved quickly. The force moved to the heights of Macantene on 21 July, incomprehensibly without resistance. All was too easy. On the plain below there were five thousand hostile warriors. Mouzinho's force was arrayed in a defensive square, and as the warriors charged on foot, the two cannons discharged their grenades at 1,000 metres. As the mass of men reached a range of 400 meters, the Portuguese opened fire. When the mass had closed to 200 meters, Mouzinho and his cavalry launched a charge through an opening in the square. This bold engagement was the first and only traditional cavalry charge ever mounted in Mozambique. The intimidating nature of this horse-mounted force stupefied the enemy who disbanded and fled. In less than two hours the battle was over, and Mouzinho was enjoying lunch with his wife. Portuguese casualties were two European and three Africans killed.[43] Cavalry had carried the day.

Mouzinho departed for Lisbon on 18 November to appeal to the government for a loan to support economic expansion and reforms in the colony. He was received warmly and in April 1898 returned to Mozambique, where on 7 July he received notice that the loan had been granted. Amazingly, the next day he was relieved of his duties and later in the month proceeded to Lisbon, his dreams for the colony crushed. Tragically on 8 January 1902, he committed suicide.

Mouzinho more than any other cavalry officer at the time embodied the cavalry spirit, a blend of aggressiveness and confidence that inspired and encouraged a thrusting team energy. This spirit was not necessarily rooted in a common sporting interest in the horse, equitation, or horsemanship, but rather in the pride and love of operating as a cohesive military unit, trusted by commanders to act on its own with discretion, boldness, and initiative in finding and engaging an enemy successfully.

Despite the difficult times, in January 1902 the School was moved to its permanent home at Torres Novas, where it was close to the centres of national decision-making and consequently expanded into an important force militarily and politically. After eight years, the Republican Revolution in 1910 ousted a weakened king and installed a republic on the French model in an almost uneventful change in government. The army made no effort to save an unpopular king. Suddenly there were new service chiefs with new loyalties. With its lost patron and sponsorship, the school lost its political influence and on 24 December 1911 was reduced in name and importance to a mere School of Equitation (Escola de Equitação). The new name, however, did not reflect the actual activity at the School, which continued its important training and development of horse warfare. Just prior to this reduction in status, Portugal struggled in bringing order to its colonies in Africa and particularly the area of southern Angola. The number, fierceness, and scale of military

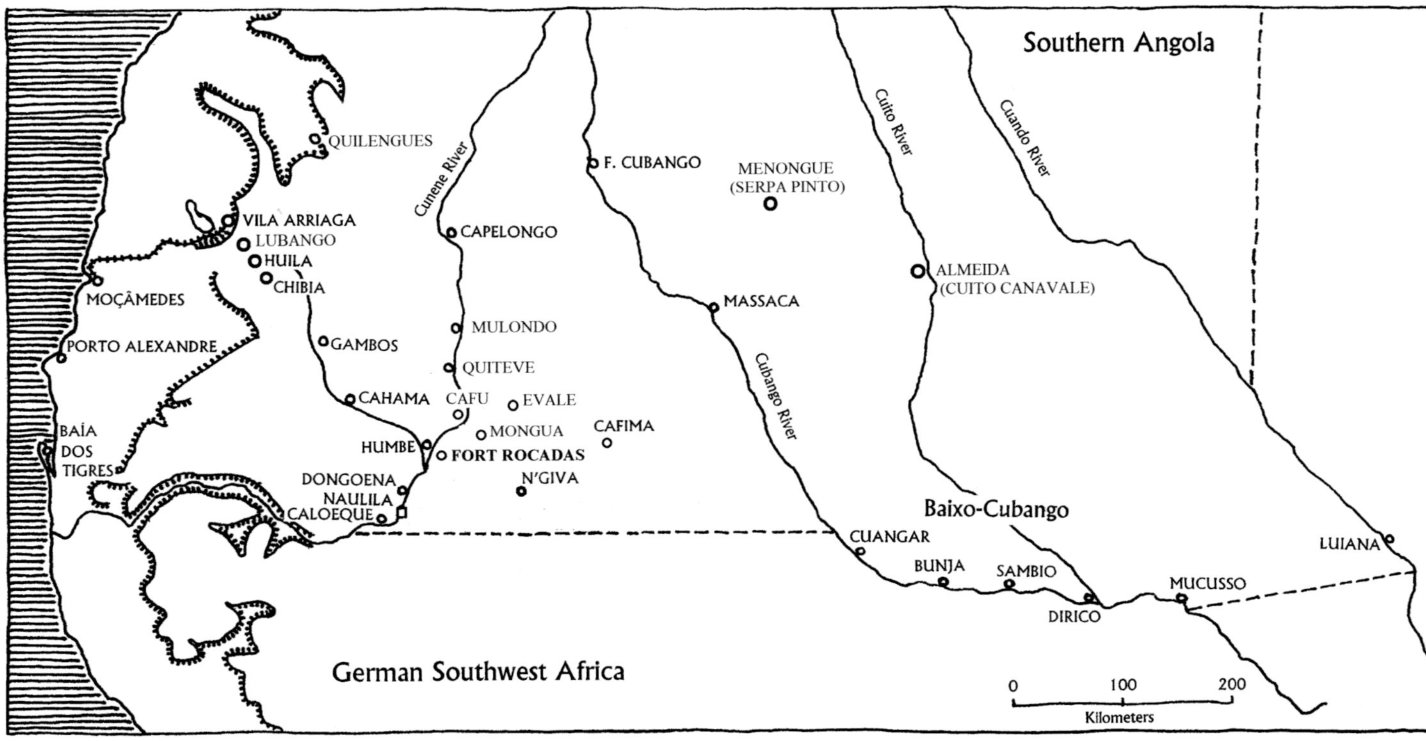

Map of Portuguese outposts in southern Angola in the early twentieth century. (Map by the author)

operations there was such that it was the only area where Portugal waged a European-style war with large troop deployments from the metrópole and the use of heavy weapons and cavalry. The area symbolised war and came to be the acid test of Portuguese colonising ability. Here the horse played an important role.

The South of Angola 1897

The Portuguese presence in the South of Angola began in 1785, when Barão de Moçâmedes attempted to colonise the coastal area around the bay named for him. He found the local people hostile, and this frustrated his efforts. In 1839 the Fort of Ponta Negra was established on the bay, and a trading post opened. These events marked the true beginning of Portuguese development of the area. As the economy around the post expanded, there was a push inland and into the highlands, and this was met with local resistance. By 1858 forts had been established at Lubango (about 70 miles inland), Gambos (about 120 miles inland), and Humbe (about 60 miles southeast of Gambos). Penetration inland, however, had been irregular and tentative because of the hostility of the local tribes. Subduing these required complicated and expensive campaigns, something that Portugal found difficult to afford and manage.

In the fall of 1897 southern Angola was hit by an epidemic that devastated the cattle herds. It had begun in the regions of Damaralândia and Ovampo of German Southwest Africa, today portions of Namibia, and moved rapidly north into southern Angola.[44] Cattle raising was the principal economic activity in this region, and the colonial administrators, aiming to halt the epidemic, initiated a campaign to vaccinate the herds against the pestilence. To assist in this project and protect the veterinary team, the local army detachment, the Company of Dragoons of the Plateau of Moçâmedes (A Companhia de Dragões do Planalto de Moçâmedes), was enlisted and sent 151 men to Humbe.[45] It was commanded by Captain José Eugénio da Silva, and its three platoon commanders were Lieutenant Conde de Almoster, Alferes Carlos Augusto de Oliveira, and Alferes Fernando Augusto da Silva Guardado.[46] The dragoons were on foot, as their mounts had died from horse sickness, a disease endemic to the plateau. The lesson of this cavalry limitation in Africa would influence later cavalry deployments.[47] Initially the local people were amenable to having their cattle vaccinated, but then the elders ruled against it, alleging that it was all a pretext to send troops, and troops only fought. It was beyond the elders' comprehension that troops might simply be additional manpower to aid in the vaccination effort in which many hands were needed. During the standoff the herds were reduced from an estimated 25,000 head to about 1,000.[48] The entire episode occurred during the rainy season, making the roads impassable with the consequence that rations for the deployed Portuguese had not kept pace with the advancing force. After watching this disaster unfold, the now useless vaccination brigade and its escort were ordered to return and began a disorderly march during which its hungry troops extorted and pillaged the villages along the way. The last platoon, which was commanded by Conde de Almoster, proceeded in a wake of ill-will and was ambushed and massacred by aggrieved locals near the village of Chicusse on 12 December 1897.[49]

Disaster at Vau de Pembe 1904

Following this massacre, the area around Humbe remained unsettled, and in September 1904 the Portuguese sent a force there to pacify the Cuamato people. The troops, plagued by dysentery and discord in their leadership, were about 500 in number, and included six platoons of dragoons.[50] The commander, Captain Pinto de Almeida, relied on a Mbundu guide from Humbe who pretended to know the countryside. He led the force in the direction of a ford (vau) across the Cunéne River near the village of Pembe and into a clearing around which the Cuamato were hidden in trees. As the Portuguese force entered the clearing, the Cuamato opened fire from their vantage. The officers in the lead died immediately. The cavalry then charged the trees, and its mounts were shot from under the troopers. Within the cul-de-sac the Cuamato unleashed a withering fire uncharacteristic of Africans and to date unknown in Angola. Sensing victory, the Cuamato charged the Portuguese forces and engaged in hand-to-hand combat. The order to withdraw was

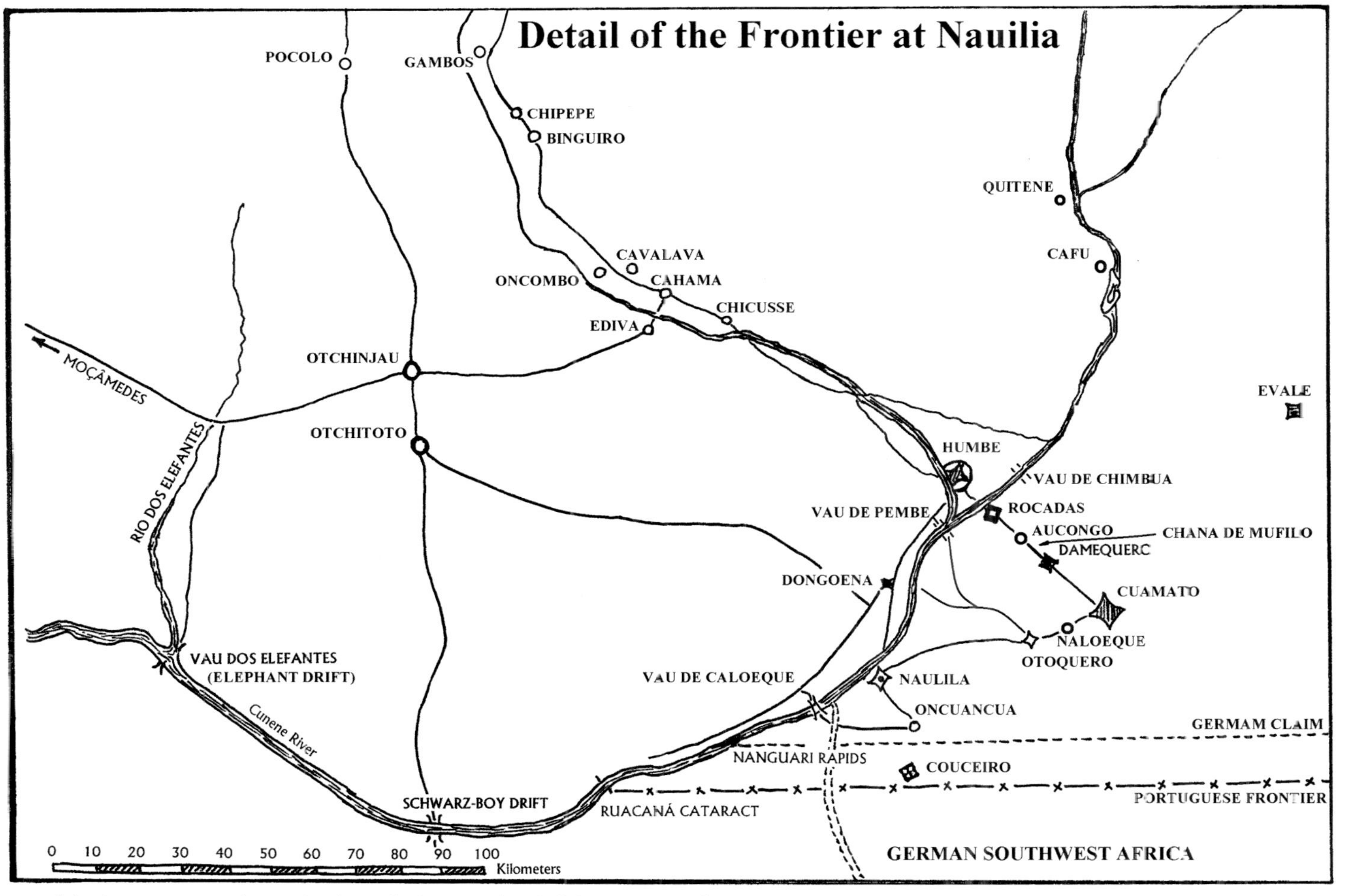

Map of the frontier area in the south of Angola showing detail of the area around Fort Naulila. (Map by the author)

given too late, and the disaster became complete. In less than two hours some 324 of the 500 Portuguese were dead, about a tenth of all forces in Angola at the time.[51] This disaster at the Vau de Pembe required a response.

The Cuamato Campaign 1907

By August 1907 a mixed force of some 2,291 men commanded by Captain José Augusto Alves Roçadas was assembled in and around Fort Roçadas, which he had built in March 1906 as a forward base southeast of Humbe. This included two squadrons of the Dragoons of Moçâmedes (Dragões de Moçâmedes). The First Squadron (1° Esquadrão) was mounted on 100 mules, and the Second (2° Esquadrão) on 95 horses and 21 mules.[52] These animals had been acquired in a purchase of 200 mules and 130 horses in

Training cavalry horses in the Bay of Moçâmedes in preparation for the Cuamato Campaign of 1907. (Archivo Histórico Militar)

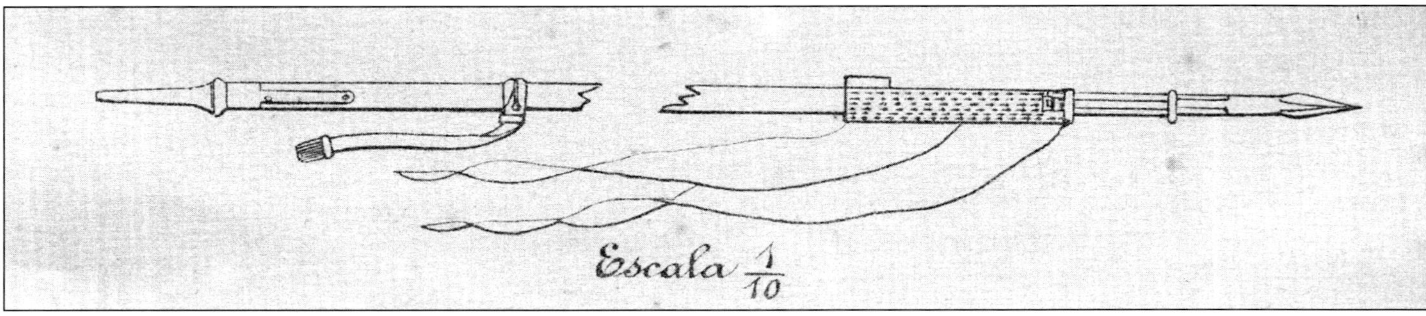

Lance that armed the Second Squadron of the Dragoons of Moçâmedes. (Archivo Histórico Militar)

Argentina and shipped to Moçâmedes, where they were mounted for the first time and together with the cavalrymen began training and instruction in tactical exercises. Argentina as a source of horses would again in the late 1960s and early 1970s supply the Portuguese in Angola with cavalry mounts. Learning from earlier experiences, great precautions were taken against horse sickness and the mite that carried it. The lance was introduced into the curriculum, and for the majority of troopers it was their first experience with the weapon.[53] The First Squadron became an escort and protection force, while the Second engaged exclusively in reconnaissance, and once contact was made, was to bring the enemy to battle. The Second, now de facto lancers, became the shock force, an innovative development in Portuguese colonial conflict.[54]

By August the force was assembled at Fort Roçadas and on the twenty-sixth sortied southeast into the Chana de Mufilo, where the Cuamato fired from the surrounding woods and from behind gigantic termite hills. Roçadas sought to deploy his artillery against the 20,000 to 25,000 Cuamato and their allies, and as he did so, and his intensity of fire increased, the enemy began to flee.[55] Roçadas then deployed his cavalry, and both squadrons engaged. With the artillery now silent, the troopers sought to clear the battlefield of enemy, who had moved and regrouped. As the Second Squadron advanced, it found itself trapped in a cul-de-sac similar to that at the Vau de Pembe and was surrounded by fire. At this point the lancers yelled, "We are surrounded, comandante! We are surrounded!" Lieutenant Alfredo Martins de Lima, their commander, without hesitation yelled to them heroically, "Solders! Our squadron when it is surrounded opens the way with the point of the lance."[56] With little alternative, the troopers charged with their lances and broke the lethal circle.[57] The Cuamato were surprised by the audacity of these Portuguese and intimidated by the charging horses and dangerous lances, as heretofore in their experience colonial forces had wilted under fire. The unnerving psychological effect of a charging horse on an infantryman would again be exploited by the Portuguese later in the century.

Roçadas then on the 28th established a fortified position at Aucongo to assure his line of communication with Fort Roçadas. Aucongo was attacked three times during the week, but in all instances the enemy was repulsed and showed a decreasing ability to annihilate the 2,000 Portuguese behind well defended fortifications.[58] On 10 September, Roçadas marched to Damequero, where again the enemy was repulsed after strong attacks. On 22 September construction was begun on Fort Dom Luís de Bragança, renamed Fort Cuamato in 1911 after the fall of the monarchy, in the centre of the Cuamato, and from the redoubt Roçadas completed their pacification. The campaign was concluded in less than two months with a loss to the Portuguese of 42 dead and 125 wounded.[59] It is estimated that the Cuamato lost 8,000 men.[60]

Naulila 1914

The vastness of Angola, the long uncontrolled southern border with German Southwest Africa, and the relatively primitive communications made it particularly vulnerable to any German incursion. In the lead-up to the First World War, Governor-General

The Second Squadron of the Dragoons of Moçâmedes wielding their lances in the Chana de Mufilo from the panel of azulejos in the Regiment of Lancers No. 2. (Regiment of Lancers No. 2)

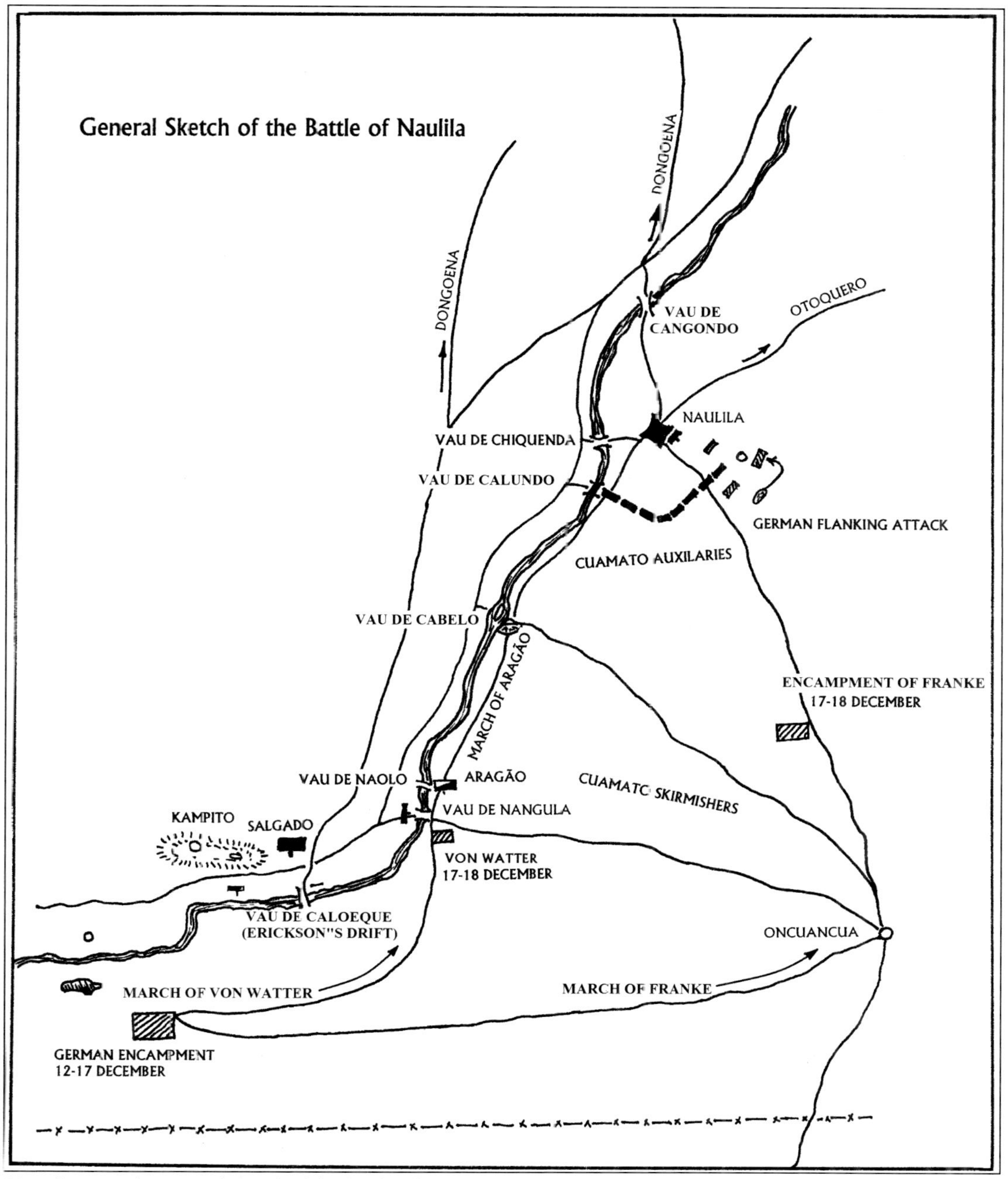

Map showing the general sketch of the battle of Naulila. (Map by the author)

Norton de Matos had few troops with which to police the frontier, much less to defend the colony, so it was not difficult to foresee trouble. As war developed in Europe in early August 1914, so there was a steady exodus of Germans from Angola, a clear indication that open hostilities were just around the corner. Portugal began the First World War as a neutral, and yet on 25 August 1914 German forces from German East Africa (today Tanzania) attacked the Portuguese outpost of Maziúa on the Rovuma River frontier in Mozambique. It quickly became apparent that Portugal was on the verge of war with Germany in the south of Angola, if not elsewhere, and Norton de Matos declared on 12 September that German troops entering the territory would be disarmed and interned.[61]

In response to this activity and the threat of local unrest among the Cuamato and Cuanhama people, Lisbon dispatched an expedition in early September under the leadership of Roçadas, now a lieutenant colonel. This force from the metrópole appeared formidable with 54 officers, 76 sergeants, and 1,395 soldiers. Additionally, there were a battery of mountain artillery, another of machine guns, and two squadrons of cavalry under the overall command of Lieutenant Francisco Xavier da Cunha Aragão.[62] The mission of this force was to occupy the area of Cuanhama and establish a series of supply depots extending along a line from Quihita to Gambos, Cahama, Fort Roçadas, and finally Fort Cuamato in anticipation of local trouble, both native and German. In augmenting these supply bases, it was also to improve the road network and the passages across the Cunéne River, mobilise local troops, selectively reinforce local outposts in the Cuanhama area, and counter any German incursions.[63] These were ambitious goals for such a force operating over a primitive infrastructure in hostile terrain and showed some naiveté, in light of the mismatch between the resources available and the tasks assigned. The expedition arrived in Moçâmedes on 1 October 1914 and over the next two months struggled with the hardships of primitive conditions in deploying to execute its plan.

In preparing for this offensive, the 1st Squadron of the Dragoons of Angola was reconstituted with 115 horses newly arrived from the Cape Colony in South Africa. This influx had overwhelmed Aragão's small contingent of eighteen cavalrymen, and as a result, by the end of the first month only four horses were in a condition to be ridden.[64] Mobilisation of the squadron moved slowly, as additional experienced cavalrymen were scarce, and the matériel issued was deficient. For example, requisitions for arms and tack were only incompletely filled, when they were filled at all. Many of the carbines delivered did not function. There were no lances available. The swords were few and old. The tack received was inadequate old, and badly worn. The saddles were poorly made, and their panels did not fit the backs of the horses well and caused wounds.[65] Makeshift stirrups wounded the horses so badly that 30 percent of the mounts were incapacitated by the time that they arrived at the Cunéne River.[66] These difficulties were reflective of the new republican government and its low priority for Africa, and all of this slowed deployment of the cavalry to the eighteen various forts and garrisons along the projected path of the force. From September there was only a single platoon deployed to Cuamato, and that was under Alferes Manuel Alvares Sereno. Despite the hurdles, Aragão, his officers, sergeants, and men were able to produce a well-trained and disciplined force, making the most of opportunities as they presented themselves.[67]

The arrival at Lubango of elements of the 1st Squadron of Dragoons, which courageously attacked the Germans on 18 December 1914. In the forefront is Lieutenant Artur Matias, the platoon leader. (Arquivo Histórico Militar)

During this time Roçadas had been assembling his force at Lubango (officially Sá da Bandeira between 1885 and 1975) and had added such colonial troops as he was able to recruit locally. His force had now more than doubled in size to 112 officers and 2,897 soldiers with nine cannon, six heavy machine guns, and his cavalry.[68] This effort had required a month and a half to complete because of ad hoc planning and a very limited infrastructure. As a result of both, there was scarcely enough fresh water, and provisions were short. In the first place, the rail line from the port of Moçâmedes to Vila Arriaga had deteriorated since its completion in 1910. There were normally four and sometimes five railcars, each with a capacity of twenty-five tons, and it required two days to travel the line and load and unload the cars.[69] This process allowed as a practical matter no more than 300 tons of material to be moved each week. As there were 1,200 tons to be moved from Moçâmedes inland, the process consumed four weeks to the rail end at Vila Arriaga and extended another two to points beyond. Further, from Vila Arriaga onward the roads were poor, there were no trucks available, the number of porters was very limited, and there were only a small number of relatively slow farm carts. The 400 kilometres from Vila Arriaga to Fort Cuamato over bad roads and under difficult conditions made the projection of Portuguese power into southern Angola slow and vulnerable. Along the way the lack of water and pasture for the animals took its toll. Disease was a constant enemy of troops and animals alike, and it was necessary to improvise with makeshift infirmaries. As 30 percent of the animals were incapacitated, one must infer through similar evidence that the troops were likewise affected.[70] Water, rations and fodder were constantly in short supply and struggled to reach the advancing column.

Major Alberto Salgado commanded the lead element of Roçadas's force with three companies of infantry, one of which was Mozambican, a battery of machine guns, an artillery battery of three cannon, and a squadron of cavalry under Aragão. Salgado reached Gambos on 6 November and paused at Oncombo on the eleventh to rest his party because of fatigue, thirst and a lack of water. From here he dispatched a company due south on the twelfth to reconnoitre possible German activity in the areas of Vau dos Elefantes (Elephant Drift), Schwartz-boy Drift, and Vau do Caloeque (Erikson Drift). He continued to advance and reached Fort Roçadas on the seventeenth. He spoke with Roçadas the next day by telephone, receiving instructions to protect Humbe and the bank of the Cunéne River from the position of Fort Cuamato. Given the health of his troops and their requirement for water, he saw this order as difficult, for the small fort with its limited facilities was some thirty kilometres from the river and would require a constant chain of carts to keep the water tanks filled. In the middle of the night of the nineteenth the commander of Fort Cuamato informed Salgado that a German column had been seen to enter Portuguese territory and appeared to be headed toward the small post of Naulila. The next morning a force of about thirty was sent to reinforce the apparent target.[71] Not since the time of the Dutch in 1641 and the French at Cabinda in 1784 had the Portuguese faced a European force in Angola.

The cavalry squadron under Aragão was deployed as a scouting force on the southern side of the Cunéne River to reconnoitre German movements. On the thirteenth Aragão in one of his patrols around Vau de Caloeque (Erikson Drift) and the German encampment captured a German soldier in a skirmish. On interrogation the prisoner revealed that the force was led by Major Erich Victor Carl August Franke, was composed of between 600 and 700 men, and Aragão was only observing the advance column. It is not known whether or not he revealed Naulila as the target.

Portuguese indecision regarding German intentions continued through the seventeenth with a series of plans and counter-plans. By early afternoon the Germans began to march eastward. News of this development was slow to reach Aragão and his cavalry, and he finally received it at 1630 hours. It now became apparent that the German force would circle the Portuguese left flank towards Aragão, who was then screening the ford of Vau de Nangula, and not cross the river, as had been anticipated. Naulila was now clearly the target.

The Germans had with them the ex-chief of the Cuamatos, Xetaquela, who had been overthrown by Roçadas in 1907 and exiled to Damaralândia. As Franke's force approached the line of Cuamato skirmishers, Xetaquela successfully appealed to them to desert and allow the Germans to pass unhindered. Aragão became aware that the Germans were passing on his left flank and guessed that they would be moving toward Oncuancua and thence to Naulila. He thus broke camp at 1930 hours and moved to intercept the force short of Naulila.

While Aragão seemed confident of the German intentions, Roçadas's headquarters appeared uncertain. It was supposed that the Cuamato skirmishers would have reported contact, if the left flank was going to be attacked. There was thus a reluctance to move additional forces towards the defence of Naulila in a vacuum of intelligence. Roçadas, indecisive, consequently waited. Aragão was an aggressive cavalry officer and sought enemy contact without orders. Even so, he was not able to establish it during the night of the seventeenth and the early morning of the eighteenth in his move north. The lack of orders to other elements, however, had a telling effect. Salgado remained guarding the fords of Vau de Caloeque and Vau de Nangula, and similar units remained isolated from the developing fight.

Franke had divided his forces in two parts, one under Captain von Watter and the other under himself. Von Watter was to advance from his bivouac south-east of Vau de Nangula northward along the bank of the Cunéne prior to daybreak on the eighteenth, and Franke would advance on Naulila from his forward encampment on the Naulila-Oncuancua road. The plan was to converge on Naulila at first light and on Franke's signal open fire simultaneously. Unfortunately, as daylight approached, it was obvious that the terrain of thick grass and rough thorn bushes made an infantry assault difficult. The fort at Naulila was well defended, and the Portuguese were ready. As the battle opened, the situation became quite confused. Franke and von Watter struggled to generate a coherent attack through the natural impediments. Artillery fire was erratic and inaccurate. The Portuguese returned the fire with some effect but were hindered by the frequent jamming of their machineguns and the poor marksmanship of the conscripts.[72] Acts of bravery were commonplace on both sides amidst the confusion, and the lines swung back and forth.

Because of the terrain Aragão could hear the battle but not fix the enemy. In ordering his attack, he moved in the direction of the fort to enter the fray. In the midst of his cavalry charge, he soon found himself in the centre of the German offensive and began to suffer casualties, himself being wounded and taken to a German aid station. Aragão survived and on his return to Lisbon in 1915 became a minor celebrity.[73] Cavalry in this case had proved valiant but unable to be decisive.

At one moment the Germans thought that they had lost the battle, but then the Portuguese were forced to evacuate their forward trenches when the local troops began to desert en masse. This move exposed their left flank. The force fell back to the seeming protection of the fort; however, German cannon and machinegun fire poured upon its mud walls designed to defend against Africans without heavy weapons and destroyed the structure wholesale. With this development, the Germans seized the opportunity and pressed their attack in an infantry charge with fixed bayonets. As the German charge came within a dozen metres of the fort, all resistance ceased. Destruction within the fort was nearly total, and the wreckage began to burn. Roçadas could have responded with his survivors, as he had the numerical advantage. His toll was heavy but not catastrophic, and this initial setback could have been overcome.[74] He chose not to do so, and thus in five and a half hours of combat the Portuguese lost both face and the fruit of their earlier pacification campaigns. The inertia and overconfidence of Roçadas was clearly responsible for this reverse. While the Germans left the scene of the battle the next day, Roçadas believed that he was pursued and abandoned any thought of returning to the offensive, for which he largely had the means. He allowed his opportunity to be swept away in the frantic stampede of his entire force. His men were demoralised by false rumours of an overwhelming German presence and fled, abandoning their weapons. The retreating troops covered the seventy kilometres between Naulila and Humbe in twenty-eight hours and left a trail of abandoned dead and dying. The chief Xetaquela was particularly pleased at the defeat of the same Roçadas who had caused him to flee seven years earlier. With Roçadas's troops in disarray, Xetaquela took advantage of the situation.

The Cuamato, who had been practically disarmed in the re-conquest of 1907, took up the abandoned arms and munitions, which included some 1.4 million small-arms rounds, and sought their revenge.[75] Naulila had become the signal for a vast uprising in southern Angola. The line of forts established in 1907 beyond Humbe were evacuated by Roçadas in great disorder: Naloéque, Otoquero, Damequero, and Cuamato were all attacked by the Cuamato. Eventually Humbe, which had been maintained at great sacrifice for half a century, was abandoned. The disaster continued with the loss of Quitene and Mulondo and stopped only at Capelongo. Further east troops abandoned Cafima for Massaca. By the end of December 1914, there was no Portuguese presence east of the Cunéne in southern Angola.

The territory had become independent again for all practical purposes, and the area beyond the outposts of the plateau was now chaotic and developing into a tragedy in the absence of any rule of law. In the vacuum of the Portuguese withdrawal, an orgy of pillage ensued. As a result of this chaos, in 1915 there was a vast famine that left the population helpless and in which it is estimated that 80,000 perished.[76] This catastrophe was to facilitate the return of Portuguese rule.

Retaking the South 1915

The disaster of Naulila had to be answered despite the enormous cost of doing so. Accordingly, General António Júlio da Costa Pereira de Eça was appointed governor-general of Angola in early 1915 and relieved General Norton de Matos on his landing in Luanda in March. Pereira de Eça assembled a force of 11,267 men, which included five squadrons of cavalry:

3rd Squadron of Cavalry Regiment No. 4,
3rd Squadron of Cavalry Regiment No. 9,
3rd Squadron of Cavalry Regiment No. 11,
1st Squadron of the Dragoons of Angola, and
2nd Squadron of the Dragoons of Angola.[77]

As before, the advantages of cavalry over natives on foot in its mobility and capabilities remained an important consideration in adding horse-mounted troops. The greatest challenge in deploying this force was the logistics needed to support it. Again, as before, hunger and thirst were to be the lot of the Portuguese, as the logistics tail proved weak, a reflection of government priorities. Facing them were some 15,000 Cuanhama and perhaps 10,000 Cuamato, hence some hard fighting on thin rations lay ahead.[78]

The general faced the same difficulties as his predecessors: projecting power across a hostile land with a disorganised and lengthy logistics tail that had great difficulty moving the volumes required to support his offensive. Again, much depended on the Moçâmedes railway, unimproved since the Naulila campaign of the previous year. The inactivity at the camp in Moçâmedes was reflective of the poor logistics and demoralising for the soldiers. Even before entering combat, hunger and thirst were prevalent.[79] Pereira de Eça established discipline and slowly advanced over the traditional route towards Humbe, which was reoccupied on 7 July without resistance. On 12 July he learned that the Germans had surrendered to the South Africans and that his forces were now entirely free to pursue pacification.

At Humbe the general split his forces into four columns: Naulila, Cuamato, Evale, and Cuanhama. The Naulila detachment was composed of cavalry and was to cross the Cunéne River at Vau de Calueque and reoccupy the ruins of Naulila.[80] From there it was to join the Cuamato detachment, which was to retake the forts of 1907.[81] The Evale detachment was to depart Capelongo for Quiteve and subdue the insurrectionists between Mulondo and Cafu, crossing the Cunéne and occupying Evale.[82] The general and his chief of staff led the Cuanhama detachment, which was to pacify country heretofore unsubdued by the Portuguese. It departed a partially rebuilt Humbe on 12 August and moved through the dry

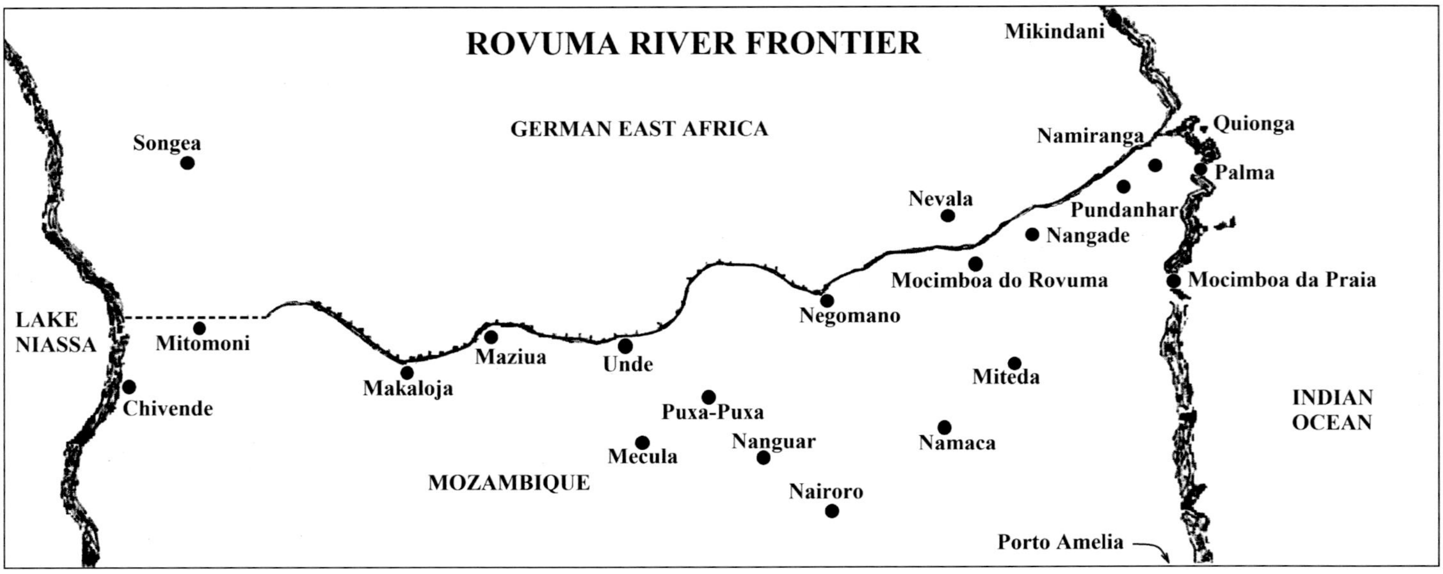

Rovuma River Outposts.(Map by the author)

chanas. Heat and thirst made progress slow, and the mules fell by the droves from exhaustion.[83] Rations and fodder were abandoned, as the pack animals succumbed. Water supplies were fragile and depended on a shuttle of wagons to the Cunéne. The Cuanhama permitted Eça to advance, as their strategy was one of attrition and relied on the heat, thirst, and difficult terrain to reduce the Portuguese. The Cuanhama concentrated their forces on the wells of Mongua, which in the dry season were the most important lands, as they contained precious water. On 17 August the Portuguese discovered the wells, and the next day a platoon probing them was attacked. The enemy was hidden behind and in the surrounding trees and opened with an intense fire, aiming at the pack animals in an attempt to immobilise the Portuguese in this semi-desert. The general, sitting astride his horse in the midst of the fray, called on his cavalry to break the encirclement, a tactic that in wooded terrain is heretical and consequently proved as unsuccessful as it was at the Vau de Pembe. Losses for the Portuguese were slight at sixteen dead, but the munitions had been squandered, and water and rations lost.

Meanwhile, the Cuamato detachment had reoccupied Fort Cuamato on 15 August without major difficulty and was now ordered to make a diversion eastward on N'Giva, the unofficial capital of the Cuanhama, to draw them away from the besieged Eça. However, in the final analysis it was not the N'Giva diversion but the bayonets of the infantry, the fuzileiros, and the Mozambicans that broke the enemy stranglehold and gained possession of his wells. In losing the water supply, the Cuanhama essentially lost the fight, as they became the target of the now Portuguese attrition strategy.

By 20 August the Cuanhama had been reinforced by allied tribes and were ready to assault the surrounded Portuguese, who pummelled them with fire from sixteen machineguns and eight cannons. As evening approached, Eça ordered infantry forays to clear his front of shooters lodged in the thickets of thornbush. After three days of repelling the Cuanhama assaults, the Portuguese were masters of the battlefield. During their defensive combat they had suffered thirty-four dead and fifty-seven wounded.[84] As always, the animals suffered the worse, as the average daily requirement for a horse under these conditions was between five and ten gallons of fresh water and about forty pounds of fodder, and these were not readily available. The results were obvious and sad, of the 445 cavalry horses with the Cuanhama detachment, only ten were capable of fighting.[85] On the advance between Humbe and Mongua 482 animals had died, and during the three days of fighting another 360 died. While the animals suffered, so did the men. Soldiers were able to drink, which saved them, but individual rations were a morsel of raw meat and a biscuit.[86] In this war of attrition there were no heroic cavalry charges, yet the mobility of the horse as basic transportation dictated large numbers. Now with the siege broken, supplies poured into the camp.

The Evale detachment had reached its goal on 21 August without firing a shot and arrived at Mongua on 27 August. As the Cuanhana and their allies fled southward, Eça paused until 2 September, when he moved his forces to N'Giva, and on the way his men burnt the abandoned Cuanhama kraals. The general now commanded some 4,000 troops in the centre of the Cuanhama. The spirit of resistance had collapsed, and Portugal terminated operations on 4 September. The old forts were rehabilitated, and any thought of African independence was extinguished for the moment.

Threat to Mozambique 1914–1918

Pereira de Eça's campaign, despite its weaknesses, accomplished its mission and was a success. Sadly, it would be some time before another campaign could boast a triumph. The politicians of the new government continued to struggle, as they developed grandiose schemes without the resources to support them. Consequently, their important military expeditions were worse than ineffective. After Macantene and the Chana de Mufilo, the cavalry entered a waning period until its recovery after the First World War. Its low points occurred in Mozambique and Europe during this war and reflect a depth of military distress and failure that prompted a much-needed change of government in 1926 and a return to sanity that led to a financial and military renaissance.

The strategic situation in Mozambique in August 1914 was driven by three factors: the progress in gaining control over the colony and its indigenous people, the means available for its defence, and the nature of the potential external threat. By 1914 Portugal effectively controlled all of Mozambique with the exception of the Maconde people in the north. This region was also where the fewest Europeans lived, where the Portuguese military had the least presence, where government administrative posts were few and scattered, and where the frontier with German East Africa was largely uncontrolled. Great portions of Mozambique were at the time managed under various agreements by several large charter companies funded by foreign capital. Of these, the Niassa Company controlled the northern portion of the colony that abutted German East Africa. Because the commercial interests of the charter companies did not necessarily coincide with the interests of the Portuguese government, the areas under contract were invariably underdeveloped, underexplored, and underpoliced. Indeed, it is said that with the arrival of the 1914 military expedition in the Niassa Company area the European population increased ten-fold.[87] Government control of northern Mozambique was thus tenuous at best, and it was vulnerable to both outside mischief and local resistance to pacification.

The troops on hand to maintain internal order and to defend the colony at this time were modest, and the initial force sent to defend the northern border in late 1914 amounted to a mere 1,539 officers and men.[88] Their effectiveness was hampered by a lack of training, poor organisation, antiquated equipment, and weak logistic support. Machine guns were few, and their artillery still contained an inventory of bronze 70mm breach-loading cannon, perhaps useful against a primitive opponent but not effective against any German invader.[89] Such a weak, unsupported force provided little security for the 900-kilometre northern border. The potential to mobilise between 5,000 and 6,000 local troops existed but was a long way from fruition.

A precursor to the nature and direction of the external threat first surfaced in 1894, when Germany crossed the Rovuma River, occupied a small area commanding its mouth that became known as the Quionga Triangle (variously Kionga Triangle), and established a customs house there.[90] Portugal was powerless to challenge this annexation. When war finally began, there were in German East Africa fourteen colonial companies each composed of about 200 askaris, indigenous African soldiers, and sixteen to twenty European officers, or a total of 260 European officers and 2,472 askaris.[91] Each company had four machine guns and 250 porters and normally operated independently, dispersed throughout the colony. This force, known as the Schutztruppe, was expanded six-fold upon wartime mobilisation to 3,007 Europeans and 12,100 askaris.[92] For a short period in the beginning, it was resupplied by sea from Germany; however, the British blockade of the German colonial ports effectively eliminated this support after April 1915.[93]

On 18 August 1914 shortly after the declaration of hostilities in Europe, Portugal made plans to dispatch its first of what would become four expeditions to Mozambique. The token expeditionary force finally left Lisbon on 11 September on the British steamship Durham Castle and arrived in Lourenço Marques on 16 October in disgraceful condition. The ship was neither properly outfitted nor serviced for carrying troops, and unhygienic conditions developed on the voyage. The force disembarked beaten and demoralised before even being deployed to the frontier. When it arrived at Pôrto Amélia, no arrangements had been made to receive the men. Consequently, the ship was forced to discharge them into the sea as close to the beach as it could safely manoeuvre. As Alberto Simões notes in his memoires:

> The ship lay at anchor at the center of the bay, static, an apocalyptic colossus, out of all proportion […] enormous blacks, naked but for a piece of cloth tied around their kidneys, entered the water, their teeth shining from open mouths, to carry men on their backs. There was some hesitation among the white troops who arrived only to be received in such grotesque fashion; but the bravest among them climbed onto the back of the blacks, while carrying their own gear, and then clung desperately to the hair of the blacks, who whined like pursued rats but who ferried them to dry land. There were no personal disasters nor forced baths. One, two, three long hours this mardi gras procession went on, to great laughter and some scares, of little consequence.[94]

Once ashore, they were quartered in makeshift native straw huts with thatched roofs over zinc sheeting. As it was the rainy season, the water penetrated the shelters and soaked everything. The entire encampment became a swamp with the area awash in manure and urine from the animals. The expedition commander observed cynically that this was the hospitality provided by the Niassa Company and the thoughtful government of Mozambique in this the twentieth century. It was said by his troops that Francisco Barreto had had a better reception in the fifteenth century with all of its hardships.[95]

This description of misery would not be complete without special attention to the fate of the horse in this setting. The horses and mules likewise arrived to an unprepared reception. In all, there were 1,500 horses – 700 from Europe and 800 from the Transvaal – and 1,000 mules on two ships.[96] By coincidence they arrived simultaneously, and this put a strain on the debarking operation. There materialised several large wooden rafts to carry the horses and mules to the beach, yet there were no paddocks, no sheds, and no one managing the situation ashore to receive these valuable animals. They were loaded onto the rafts in a precarious operation complicated by rain and wave action, and when they arrived at the beach, many were lost into the remoteness of the countryside because of a lack of facilities. These either died of hunger, or were eaten by lions, or succumbed to trypanosomiasis from the tsetse fly bite.[97] At the end of the multi-year campaign even the survivors would be abandoned and left in Africa, a sad waste for which no one appeared to assume responsibility.

After four centuries of African expeditions, it was difficult to believe the distress of the expedition. The entire foray had been assembled on impulse with little preparation. No amount of experience in expeditionary warfare, knowledge of Africa, or intelligence on the enemy seemed to have served this expedition, and Portugal had acquired a wealth over time in all three.[98] An expeditionary force is generally designed to be largely self-sufficient and tends to bring with it most of its requirements. As such, it is self-reliant, self-sustaining, and adaptable to the most austere environments. This expedition was little more than a handful of sick soldiers dumped into a hostile setting with little support. Not only was there a lack of preparation and provisions, but also during its ten-month tenure it continually received conflicting instructions from Lisbon and the colonial governor.[99] The result was a difficult start and modest accomplishment. On top of these problems, there was no well-defined mission other than to provide a mild deterrent presence. Portuguese strategic goals were thus not translated into operational and tactical actions that would support national policy. Had Portugal thoughtfully considered the situation in East Africa, then it would have deployed a force that could have been a threat to Germany and not a danger to itself. Deployment should have been in such numbers and with such support as to defend Mozambique properly and help provide an encirclement of the German colony through coordination with the British, notwithstanding Portugal's neutral status. Sadly, this sort of irresponsible administration became a trademark of the new republican government. The lack of resources inherent in this venture was to plague subsequent expeditions and undermined the entire Portuguese war effort in East Africa. At the end of the fourth expedition in March 1918, its commander notified the governor-general that there was a shortage of money and medicines, that his hospitals were full to overflowing with the sick and wounded, that there was no transportation for their evacuation, and that there was little food. The local soldiers were deserting because they could not be paid or fed. The governor-general's reply is not recorded.[100]

The Portuguese experience in East Africa during this period was a needless tragedy. Of the approximately 13,453 men sent to Mozambique between 1916 and 1918, 143 died in combat and 3,556 died of disease, a mortality rate of 27.5 percent.[101] Only 307 were wounded.[102] There were no inspirational cavalry charges, and man and beast suffered needlessly. After ousting the monarch in 1910, the politicians of the new republican government authored a spiral of economic disaster. The army was thus without proper funding, and robbed of this wherewithal, experienced a severe decay. It was in no way ready to go to war and, when it did, was never given the opportunity to succeed. It could not fight effectively without proper training, modern weapons, and appropriate logistic support, and these were denied it. General Manuel Gomes da Costa justly accuses his political leaders of being intellectually barren and of allowing the army's best men to be sacrificed needlessly.[103] There is clearly ample blame to be shared among the politicians and generals for the flawed strategies that caused so much tragedy in East Africa. Yet, there was additional malfeasance.

The CEP and The Great War 1916–1918

In 1917, after the unfortunate experiences in Angola and Mozambique, the government of Prime Minister Afonso Costa believed that only Britain could protect Portuguese Africa from the predations of Germany, even though the price to be paid was the raising of an expeditionary force to replace the enormous Allied losses in France. This was a misguided and ruinous decision and was to yield little at the peace negations considering the sacrifice. Nevertheless, in August 1916 Portugal began to assemble and train an expeditionary force centred at Tancos, which it called the Corpo Expedicionário Português (CEP). This project strained the entire military infrastructure, as there were inadequate barracks, food, water, uniforms, and arms to accommodate the 20,000 men assembled. Between January and September 1917 in successive waves the CEP was prepared and transported to Brest by ship and then by train to its assignment near the front lines. Following a period of adaptation under British tutelage, the CEP was installed next to British troops in a sector in French Flanders opposite the city of Lille between Armentières and Bétaune. Ultimately the CEP consisted of some 55,000 troops, which initially included a cavalry group of two squadrons. They were unsuitable to the combat environment in Flanders, where the horses were completely vulnerable to machinegun and artillery fire, and consequently the entire cavalry group was converted to a bicycle infantry battalion called the Group of Cyclist Companies (Grupo de Companhias de Ciclistas). Such cyclist troops had their origin in the nineteenth century with the popularity of the bicycle, and while its notion as an engine of war was a particularly British one, France, Italy, and Germany had experimented with the concept prior to the war.[104] In the British case, which was the model for the Portuguese cavalry conversion, cyclist units were used largely as dispatch riders and scouts. British units had trained on the developed infrastructure of the British Isles road system and demonstrated good mobility in this medium; however, when in Flanders, cyclist troops proved far less able, as the roads were largely mud trails or fields. In this combat environment tyre blowouts, uninviting terrain, and enemy fire substantially reduced cycling capability. The advantage of bicycle speed over that of a man on foot was negated, and the cycle was unable to realise its potential.

While the bicycle could be disassembled and carried, this did not improve mobility. Further, a rider could not shoot from a bicycle as well as he could from a horse, as he could use both hands from horseback while he steered his mount with his knees. Transporting heavy loads, such as a machinegun, likewise proved infeasible on a bicycle. The European battlefield of the First World War simply was not the combat environment that favoured either the bicycle

Portuguese cavalry exercising at Tancos in preparation for deployment to France as part of the Portuguese Expeditionary Corps, known by its acronym CEP (Corpo Expedicionário Português). (Photo by Joshua Benoliel, 1916, Arquivo Municipal de Lisboa)

or the horse. It did not favour man either, as of the approximately 55,000 Portuguese troops deployed to France during the war, the CEP suffered about 2,515 deaths from combat, over 5,000 wounded in combat, over 7,000 rendered incapable of fighting due to illness, and 6,678 taken prisoner.[105] Sadly, this sacrifice yielded only crumbs at the Versailles Peace Conference of 1919.

It should be noted that despite the introduction of the machinegun, cavalry was successfully deployed in the Middle East theatre of the war by the Australian Mounted Division against Ottoman Empire forces and their German advisors at Beersheba, Ottoman Syria, in 1917. After the war, however, cavalry was largely relegated to ceremonial duties and certainly so with most modern armies. Even so, in Portugal cavalry training continued its proud tradition.

The Interwar Years

While the European war yielded little for the School in Torres Novas, Africa was another story. With the exception of the four First World War expeditions to Mozambique and the disaster at Naulila, cavalry units had proved themselves in Africa, and this theatre became the focus of the School. In 1918 Lieutenant Colonel António Óscar de Fragoso Carmona, a career cavalry officer, became commandant of the School and introduced a period of great dynamism amid sizable demands. A look at the training routine at the School under his leadership is worthwhile.

At Torres Novas the training was exhausting for a cavalryman with the early rising and grooming of his horse. He became intimately familiar with its saddling and feeding, checking its fetlocks and hooves, stroking its withers, and talking to it in gentle tones. This grooming and loving care, the routine of so many mornings, reassured the animals. This was followed by group riding exercises day after day: loping, trotting, cantering, and galloping. Then it was formation exercises: learning to ride in a squadron formation and to manoeuvre it. This last culminated in learning to charge and hold formation doing so.

The horses themselves made the long training hours a joy, and soon the cavalryman became one with his horse. Troopers learned to vault onto their mounts, slip onto the side of their horses, and shoot over their backs. They also learned to order the horses to lie on their sides so that the troopers could rest their rifles on the horses' flanks. Marksmanship was very important and shooting accurately from horseback at a gallop was considered the ultimate skill.

The School assembled and trained units at an accelerated rate and sent them abroad on numerous military missions. The prestige of the School consequently expanded substantially, and Carmona was promoted to colonel while there. When he departed in 1922, the major African pacification campaigns had been largely completed, and there was a consequent slackening of the training tempo at the School. In 1925 the name was again changed to the School of Cavalry Employment (Escola de Aplicação Cavalaria) in light of the new mechanised battlefield developments. The next year during the Revolution of 28 May 1926, when the military intervened and attempted to end an era of irresponsible government, the school was returned to its earlier name of the Practical School of Cavalry and subjected to modernising reforms in light of the development of armoured vehicles.

The primary concern of the military in its assumption of governing responsibility in 1926 was to restore order in the streets and fiscal discipline and confidence in the government. The generals were able to restore civil order but were unable to solve the underlying fiscal problem. To help with this they called on

Cavalry trooper at the Practical School of Cavalry with his mount lying on his side in a position that allows him to rest his rifle on the horse's body when shooting. (Photograph by José Carreira, 1st Sergeant, Practical School of Cavalry at Torres Novas, 1943)

Horses at the Practical School of Cavalry paired in close formation with troopers standing with a foot on the saddle of each to demonstrate the high degree of formation discipline. (Photograph by José Carreira, 1st Sergeant, Practical School of Cavalry at Torres Novas, 1943)

Troopers at the Practical School of Cavalry standing on the saddles of their mounts at a trot. (Photograph by José Carreira, 1st Sergeant, Practical School of Cavalry at Torres Novas, 1943)

an obscure economics professor at the University of Coimbra, António de Oliveira Salazar. Salazar came to Lisbon and took a look at the financial situation, at which time he told the generals that

Dual mount jumping at the Practical School of Cavalry. (Photograph by José Carreira, 1st Sergeant, Practical School of Cavalry at Torres Novas, 1943)

Trooper at the Practical School of Cavalry demonstrating the use of his mount as a shield from enemy fire. (Photograph by José Carreira, 1st Sergeant, Practical School of Cavalry at Torres Novas, 1943)

he could not solve the problem unless he had complete control over government finances. This the generals refused, and Salazar returned to Coimbra. After a period of struggle, the generals again turned to Salazar, and in 1928 he agreed to become Finance Minister under the assurance that he would have a free hand in vetoing expenditures throughout the government. Within a year Salazar balanced the budget and stabilised the Portuguese escudo, restoring order to national accounts and producing the first of many surpluses – an unparalleled novelty in Portugal. In 1933, when Salazar was appointed prime minister, and the military returned the government

A cavalry squad at the Practical School of Cavalry descending a stairway at speed. (Photograph by José Carreira, 1st Sergeant, Practical School of Cavalry at Torres Novas, 1943)

to civilian control, the name Practical School of Cavalry remained.

Between the end of the First World War and the beginning of the Second World War the cavalry forces of the industrialised European powers traded the horse for armoured cars, and the sword and lance for automatic weapons. Mechanical reliability was improving to the point that such vehicles with their mobility, protective armour, and lethal machineguns and canon were seen clearly as more capable and less vulnerable than traditional horse-mounted cavalry. For Portugal, the School remained faithful to the traditional model, strongly linked to the horse and the handling of the sword. In practice, this was an obsolete cavalry that would have no part in the Second World War. This is not to say that Portugal did not acquire some armoured vehicles, but they were not immediately integrated into its order of battle. The first vehicles came from France in 1926 and then the United Kingdom in 1928 but were not assigned to the School at the time. However, from the point of view of appraising the new weapons systems and experimenting with their potential use in combat, the School was the ideal place, as it was responsible for the practical instruction in arms.

While the School continued to teach the employment of the horse, World War Two definitively demonstrated that the speed, potency, and security of mechanised and armoured vehicles that characterised industrialised warfare was the wave of the future and would usher in a new form of cavalry far removed from the horse. By 1943 the Practical School of Cavalry had received its first mechanised matérial. By the following year there was a cavalry squadron based on the British Humber armoured car, and the school expanded into a new facility in Entroncamento and

Troopers at the Practical School of Cavalry demonstrating a stream crossing with entry from a steep bank. (Photograph by José Carreira, 1st Sergeant, Practical School of Cavalry at Torres Novas, 1943

Trooper at the Practical School of Cavalry taking a hedge and bar jump. (Photograph by José Carreira, 1st Sergeant, Practical School of Cavalry at Torres Novas, 1943)

considered additional dependencies. The US White M3 scout car was added in 1946, and the British Valentine Mk III and the Italian B1 Centauro tank, in 1948. The successive reforms centred on the acquisition of these vehicles and led to an abrupt revolution in Portuguese cavalry forces. The emphasis was now on the technical skills associated with the vehicles and their operation. Following the entry of Portugal into NATO as a founding member in 1949, more modern vehicles arrived in the form of the M47 Patton tank from the United States, and this prompted the establishment of a new Centre for Tank Instruction (Centro de Instrução de Blindados) and a school associated with it. The space required for the operation of and training with these new vehicles forced the cavalry to expand additionally to Santa Margarida. By 1953 the traditional cavalry unit had been converted to armour, while the lancers had been converted into military police.[106] There now remained only about fifty horses at the Military Academy (Academia Militar) producing aspirant officers. In 1957 the Practical School of Cavalry moved into its new quarters at Santarém, where there would be a new life for the school

Troopers at the Practical School of Cavalry taking a series of jumps in sequence. (Photograph by José Carreira, 1st Sergeant, Practical School of Cavalry at Torres Novas, 1943)

in the old Convent of Trindade, which had formerly housed the Regiment of Cavalry No. 4 and the Regiment of Artillery No. 6.

Between 1961 and 1974 the school would be affected by the new requirements for the war in Africa and would send units to all three of the theatres: Angola, Guiné, and Mozambique. These would be as light infantry in battalion-sized units and independent companies (batalhão de cavalaria), as armoured reconnaissance companies in company-sized units (esquadrão de reconhecimento), and as military police in company-sized units (companhia de polícia militar).[107] Those based on armoured vehicles would not always be useful in the African environment. Fortunately, alongside the new, Portugal did not lose touch with the traditional model strongly linked to the horse and the skills of fighting from horseback in the modern era. From 1966 onward Portugal began to test experimental units that would make effective use of the horse-mounted soldier in the east of Angola in a war often depicted as a series of mechanised infantry operations. The effectiveness of horse-mounted patrols in counterinsurgency surprised many as an old solution to an old problem.

Why the Horse?

The Portuguese experience with horse cavalry in Africa, while irregular, showed from its first deployment in the sixteenth century that the horse had many advantages over other forms of transportation under certain conditions, as we have seen, and was employed there historically on a regular basis. In an environment, such as the elevated chanas of eastern Angola, a tsetse-free area, the horse held great potential. These are largely flat plains broken by thickets of trees and scrub plants and crossed by meandering streams that can become impassable in the rainy season. They are mostly an endless wilderness of high grass. The horizon is interminable. The horse's promise as a means to police such areas against hostile activity lay in a number of factors:

First, in the immensity of the chanas the horse could provide basic transportation. Moreover, it had a versatility in negotiating varied, rough, and inaccessible terrain, such as crossing streams and moving across irregular ground, and could do so with relative ease during daylight. Cavalry operations are not conducted at night. He could cover between eight and thirteen kilometres an hour, depending on the terrain, or about fifty kilometres a day when patrolling, which with his speed and endurance was many times that of a man on foot.[108]

Second, the horse moved through the African bush in relative silence with a heightened sensory perception. This rested on the relationship between horse and rider, an empathy that enabled the

Trooper at the Practical School of Cavalry demonstrating the capability of jumping from a steep bank. (Photograph by José Carreira, 1st Sergeant, Practical School of Cavalry at Torres Novas, 1943)

rider to interpret the unique nuances of his mount. For instance, the sudden turning of a horse's head with ears pricked and a shortened stride alerts the rider to something unusual from that direction, perhaps danger. A horse pricking his ears in a specific direction and refusing to move forward definitely signals a warning. Such signals and the silent movement of the horse enabled a platoon of dragoons to surprise an enemy, an important advantage in any combat.[109]

Third, the horse provided his rider with an elevated position that would be ideal for observation in the tall grass of the chanas and would enable him to enjoy a perspective unavailable to a foot soldier. Mounted troops could see over the vegetation and undergrowth and identify insurgents readily from this vantage. It was very difficult for insurgents to ambush a patrol, as they were on foot and unable to see the horsemen well enough through the tall elephant grass for surprise. Indeed, the rider had the advantage in that he could view disturbances in the grass and follow an enemy trail, tracking an enemy effectively and achieving surprise himself.[110]

Fourth, the superior height of the trooper over an insurgent on foot was very frightening to any foe. Enemy on foot were not normally prepared to stand in the face of a charging horse with its rider firing at them, however inaccurately and despite the large target of horse and rider, as we have seen at Macantene and in the Chana de Mufilo. It was not only psychologically intimidating to a foe, but it was physically dangerous.[111]

Lastly, Portuguese horse cavalry had a long and proud tradition – a cavalry spirit, if you will, with its set of heroes in such personalities as Augusto Mouzinho de Alberquerque, Alfredo Martins de Lima, and Francisco Aragão. Mobile warfare was their game, and they played it extraordinarily well. These characteristics of mobility, surprise, visibility, intimidation, and spirit provided clear potential advantages for cavalry operating in the wide expanses of Angola and Mozambique, and as we shall see, traditional horse cavalry was to prove an effective force in the old form of warfare practiced in the twentieth century.

2
THE CHANAS OF ANGOLA

Beginning in 1947 with the independence of India, Great Britain began the dissolution of its Empire. After two unsatisfactory colonial wars, one in Indochina and the other in Algeria, France dismantled its Empire. Portugal was now the remaining colonial power. Its position was very different from Britain and France in that it had been in Africa since the beginning of the fifteenth century, over four and a half centuries and longer by far than any other colonial power. It considered the ultramar to be an integral part of continental Portugal and refused to consider granting independence to any portion of it. Commitment to its defence had its origins not only in their long-term ownership but also in their economic promise and Salazar's inflexible position on the ownership of Portuguese Africa. For this small European nation, the importance of its colonies was captured in an editorial by Marcello Caetano in *O Mundo Português* (Portuguese World) that appeared in 1935: "Africa is for us a moral justification and a raison d'être as a power. Without it we would be a small nation; with it, we are a great country."[1]

The growth of revolutionary climate in the ultramar during the 1950s clashed with this philosophy and the country's refusal to break the colonial bond and to decolonise. The "winds of change" were blowing through Africa, but the Salazar regime refused to be swayed.

Political opposition to Salazar and his policies was tolerated neither at home nor in the ultramar. Thus, an explosion was inevitable, and when it happened in 1961, the events in Angola and the seizing of Goa by India pushed Salazar to solidify the Portuguese commitment to defend the remaining colonies. So strong was this feeling that it defied any voice of reason and foreclosed any retreat over African affairs. The Portuguese armed forces and treasure were thus pledged in full to preserve its Empire and the potential of renewed prosperity through an expensive military campaign that began in Angola.

Angolan Nationalist Movements

Following the Second World War, nationalist sentiments in Angola grew among the mestiços (mixed-race peoples) and assimilados (mostly mestiços who were legally assimilated into Portuguese culture). However, these groups were largely urban and thus did not represent the greater population. As they were located in cities, they were in a hostile environment for two reasons: the majority of their opponents, the white population, lived in cities, and the national police or PIDE (Polícia Internacional de Defesa do Estado, or International Police for Defence of the State) operated most effectively there. Consequently, they were either short-lived or dormant.[2] By 1956 the young Marxists of the Angolan Communist Party contributed to the formation of the MPLA (Movimento

António de Oliveira Salazar (Nova Arrancada)

Holden Roberto (Albert Grandolini Collection)

Popular de Libertação de Angola, or Popular Movement for the Liberation of Angola). The MPLA developed roots among the urban and largely radical intellectuals of Luanda, among its slum dwellers, and to a lesser extent, eastward from the capital among the Mbundu, the second largest ethnolinguistic group in Angola, and the Chokwe people. These urban roots were composed largely of mestiços, who controlled the party. The movement had little in common with the rural peasants of the east and south of Angola and made little effort to gain their true devotion. In December 1956 the initial MPLA manifesto was openly published in a direct frontal assault on the government. Predictably the PIDE reacted adversely, and a number of the MPLA leaders were forced to flee into exile. From 1957 onward PIDE action was so successful "that the nationalists were not able to maintain more than the most rudimentary organisation inside the colonies and could not communicate with those cells that did exist."[3] The parties were forced to conduct their affairs from neighbouring states and were deeply influenced by their foreign connections.

The MPLA in exile established itself initially in Léopoldville but found itself in competition with the other prominent Angolan nationalist group at the time, the UPA (Uniao das Populações de Angola, or Union of Angolan Peoples), for acceptance as the leading representative of the Angolan people. The UPA was formed by Barros Nekaka in the mid-1950s from a number of small groups, and in 1958 he passed leadership to his nephew Holden Roberto. UPA strength rested in the rural populations of the Bakongo ethnolinguistic region of northern Angola. These people straddled the border area that reached into the Belgian Congo, Angola, Cabinda and the French Congo, the footprint of the ancient Kongo kingdom. Roberto unequivocally held the view that not just a "Bakongo kingdom" or some other entity but all of Angola must be freed. An ardent anticolonialist, Roberto had been born in Angola but had lived his adult life in the Belgian Congo. He had been educated in the Baptist Church missionaries and employed in the Belgian colonial economy as an accountant between 1941 and 1949.

The UPA was able to develop a following in the north of Angola because of the relatively open frontier, and this loyal cadre became the basis for the uprising in March 1961, of which we will hear more shortly. Portuguese presence in this area took the form of chefes do posto (heads of posts) and administrators, as opposed to PIDE, and these officials were so sparse that it was physically impossible for them to maintain anything but the most casual control over their districts.[4]

When the Belgian Congo became independent on 30 June 1960, its new government began to give Roberto practical assistance, including permission to establish a radio station and a training camp within its borders. This sanctuary was an important facet of UPA operations in its early years. Roberto had witnessed the long series of Congolese crises that had begun with the violent political rioting on 4 January 1959 and had led to the accelerated Belgian push toward Congo self-government and independence in eighteen months. By December 1960, he believed that just as the Belgians had quickly grown weary of armed conflict, so would the Portuguese when it was initiated. He consequently used his Congo sanctuary and the porous common border to set the stage for an end to relative colonial tranquillity for Portugal.

Assault on the North

The UPA assault on the north of Angola occurred primarily in the districts of Zaire, Uíge, and Cuanza Norte. The first two are next to the border, and the third abuts the other two and contains the impenetrable Dembos region, a mountainous jungle area where UPA elements hid and prepared for the internal assault. During the weeks leading to 15 March, the UPA carefully prepared its assault plan, infiltrating agitators from the Congo. It assembled its forces not only on the frontier and in the Dembos but also in many different locales within the targeted regions and was able to do so largely in secret because of the remoteness of the area and the uncontrolled borders.[5]

The order to attack was described in a pamphlet widely disseminated to the population and marked the "beginning of the festival" as 15 March.[6] It cryptically ordered all those "followers to clean all postos thoroughly, and to treat the chefs de posto and their families and other whites well," and only some days later was the hostile intent of this message understood by the Portuguese authorities.[7] Another UPA document dated March 1961, Léopoldville, and titled "Rules to Follow for the Population of Angola in the Days of the Feast," reinforces the festival pamphlet and outlines specific procedures to be followed in the "celebrations."[8] It talks about women and children leaving their villages to participate in the celebrations, soldiers and sepoys allying with the people and joining the celebrations, and all people uniting in the success of the celebrations. The "celebrations," of course, were the intended acts of mayhem to destroy the agricultural commerce of the area and important communications infrastructure. These acts were described as "cleaning the farms" and the "destruction of bridges." The underlying logic in this plan was deeply flawed in that the population that was supposed to rise up and join the UPA forces depended for its survival on the prosperity of the farms and estates and the ability of these enterprises to get their crops to market by way of the interconnecting infrastructure. Thus, despite their grievances, the resident population's loyalties could never ultimately lie with the UPA in this venture, and the people knew it.

The attacks were launched on signal, and the UPA attackers—an armed mob estimated to be 4,000 to 5,000 and drugged with quimbombo or cacharama, a native alcoholic drink and hyperstimulant, and convinced that they were immune to the

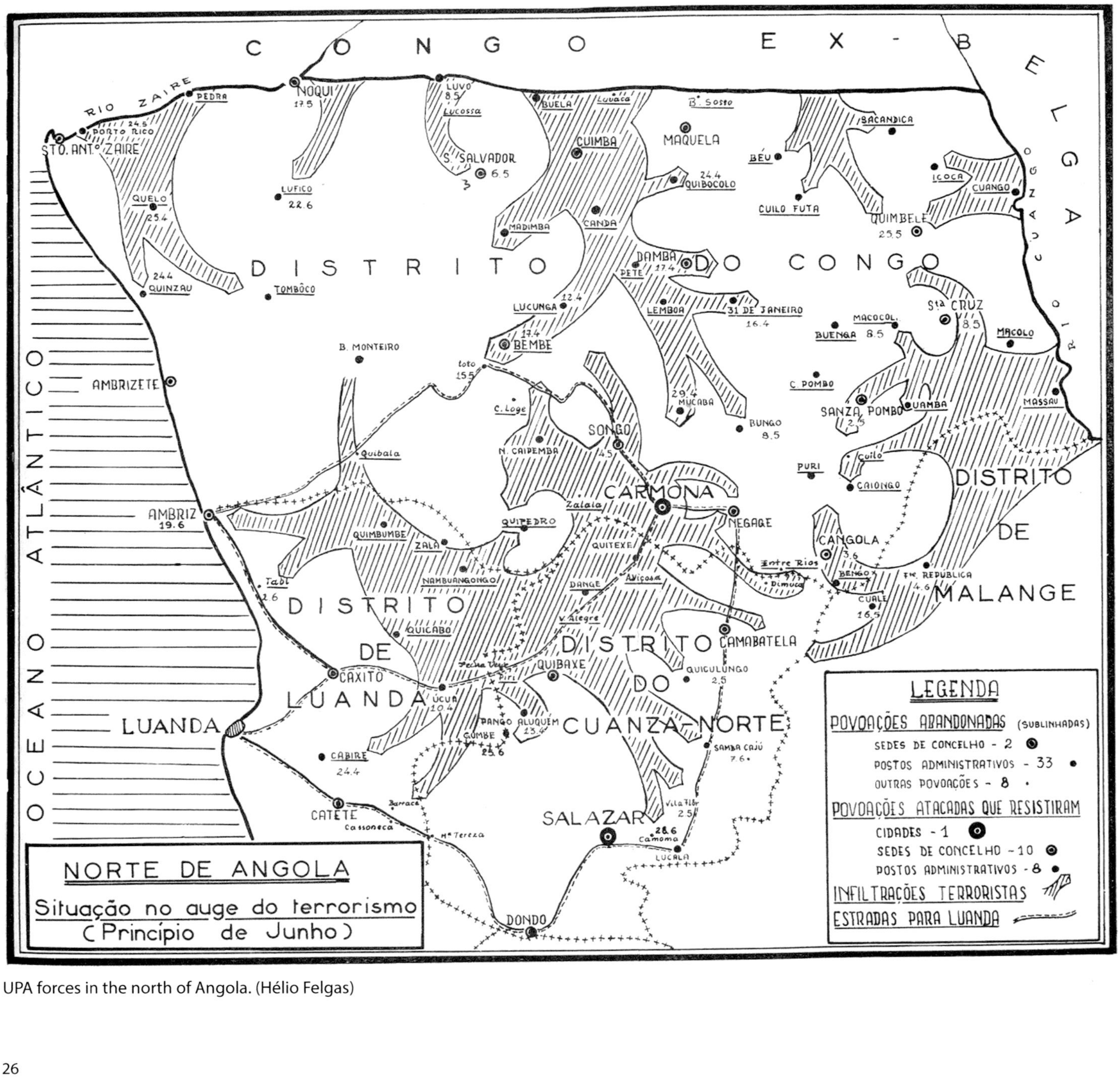

UPA forces in the north of Angola. (Hélio Felgas)

white man's bullets—swarmed from their redoubts in the Congo, the Dembos, and elsewhere in the early morning hours of 15 March.[9] This figure was expanded by an estimated 25,000 through forced recruiting.[10] From the Congo, they crossed the border at approximately seven points along a 300-kilometre front in the area of São Salvador and moved south. Approximately 700 European farms and estates, additional trading settlements, and over 100 government administrative posts were overwhelmed.[11] The mob acted with refined cruelty in massacring men, women, black, white, young, and old. At 1230 hours on that day, Radio Brazzaville announced that "the rebel forces of the UPA had begun the fight for the independence of Angola, having decimated hundreds of whites."[12] At the same time that the sad news became known in Lisbon, there was great satisfaction in its receipt at UN headquarters in New York. The Brazzaville delegate announced news of the "revolt," and immediately afterwards, the Liberia delegate made the motion to condemn Portugal for defending itself and taking measures to restore order.[13]

All of Portugal was shocked at the horror. It has been estimated that 500 Europeans and about 20,000 local people died in this jacquerie.[14] The enemy was forced to act against the greater part of the native population that remained faithful to the Portuguese. Moreover, in this assault there were clear acts of intertribal rivalry. In the north on the farms and estates there was a demand for labour to harvest crops, and these jobs were largely filled by Bailundo people from the south of Angola. While UPA forces were initially friendly to the Bailundos, after 7 April, when the enemy began burning the farms as well as the towns of Santa Isabel and Vista Alegre, these migrants began to fight the invaders.[15] As it turned out, the Bailundo workers were intensely loyal, and many died in an attempt to defend themselves, their employers, and Portugal against the UPA.[16]

For a month Portugal and Angola seemed paralyzed and unable to act. Equally, the insurgents were incapable of sustained military engagement. Civil militias were formed, and loyal Africans armed. It was this patchwork of civil-military defence and its frenetic activity that brought UPA momentum to a halt. In these initial months, the primary mission of the locally available Portuguese troops was to defend or rescue the threatened population in the three districts of Zaire, Cuanza Norte, and Uíge. This area was roughly the size of continental Portugal.

Formal military reoccupation began on 13 May and was intensified as troops arrived from the metrópole. During the July-August period approximately 20,000 reinforcements landed in Angola, and the fighting to regain the lost territory drove over 150,000 refugees into the Congo over the next nine months.[17] On 7 October, General Venâncio Augusto Deslandes, the governor-general, announced that reoccupation was complete and that mop-up policing would begin.[18] These events had deeply shocked all of Portugal and hardened its colonial commitment to the restoration of order in Angola. To the Portuguese it was unthinkable that such lawlessness should be tolerated, and a strong, uncompromising reaction to the nationalist behaviour was widely supported.

Stalemate

The UPA formed its military wing, the ELNA (Exército de Libertação Nacional de Angola, or Army of National Liberation of Angola), in June 1961 after the March attacks did not achieve a Portuguese withdrawal. It proved a relatively ineffective force, and the South African Defence Force vice-consul in Luanda, Brigadier Willem S. van der Waals, noted that the ELNA "involved itself in military activities in the narrowest sense … but avoided contact with the Portuguese security forces as far as possible."[19] Van der Waals further argues that in the traditional exercise of the informational lever of national power, Portuguese propaganda and social work among the refugees returning to Angola after the March 1961 attacks persuaded most of these displaced people to move into controlled settlements or aldeamentos. This development deprived the ELNA of popular support, and its military action consequently occurred in a human desert. It was thus unable to proselytise the population, as in a classic insurgency, and as an alternative focused on preventing competitive MPLA infiltration. It had also neglected to indoctrinate, organise, and win recruits among refugees in the Congo returning to Angola and had thus missed an important opportunity to undermine Portuguese authority. Thus, despite its expansion to 6,200 troops, the ELNA had no internal political infrastructure in Angola.[20] Portugal gained the upper hand and dominated the human terrain until 1974 in a classic example of successful informational warfare with civil support and population reassurance.

This lack of direction caused great rifts in the UPA leadership. Despite the UPA reorganisation in March 1962 at the behest of Joseph-Désiré Mobutu, the new president of the Republic of the Congo, to include additional groups, to rename itself FNLA (Frente Nacional de Libertção de Angola, or National Front for the Liberation of Angola), and to establish a government in exile named GRAE (Governo da República de Angola no Exílio, or Government of the Republic of Angola in Exile), little of substance was accomplished. A frustrated Jonas Savimbi, Roberto's "foreign minister" and an Ovimbundu, formally broke with the UPA/FNLA in July 1964, labelling Roberto a "corrupt racist," and eventually formed the third nationalist movement in Angola, UNITA (União Nacional para a Independência Total de Angola, or the National Union for the Total Independence of Angola). Savimbi had publicly announced his break at the 1964 Organisation of African Unity (OAU, now the African Union or AU) meeting in Cairo, Egypt, and alleged that Roberto had set up a "commercial empire in the Congo."[21] Within two years, Savimbi had built his meagre twelve-man force into a sizeable army, gaining popularity and support as the only leader to work within the country alongside his men in battle against the Portuguese. "Leaders must fight alongside the people and not stay abroad, sending 'second-class' fighters to face the Portuguese," Savimbi proclaimed as he denounced Roberto.[22] While Roberto was renowned for his aloofness, the bearded Savimbi mixed often and easily with ordinary people as well as his military. The next year Alexandre Taty, "minister of armaments," after challenging Roberto

Joseph-Déseré Mobutu. (Hulton Archive)

Joseph Savimbi. (Albert Grandolini Collection)

in an unsuccessful coup, defected to the Portuguese in Cabinda with a substantial number of his followers.

As the Portuguese weekly Expresso observed in 1974, "The FNLA is Holden Roberto and Holden Roberto belongs to Mobutu, to whom he is connected by an umbilical cord."[23] Throughout the war Mobutu played both ends against the middle in loudly proclaiming his support for the UPA/FNLA while discretely cultivating good relations with Portugal, for like Zambia, the Congo depended on the Benguela Railroad (Caminho de Ferro de Benguela or CFB), which carried more than half of Congolese foreign trade. The CFB connected the Atlantic port of Lobito through the eastern border town of Teixeira de Sousa and to the rail networks of south-eastern Congo and Zambia, which led to vast and rich copper mines. There were also dissident elements in Angola that, if unleashed in cross-border operations, could make considerable trouble for him. Consequently, he kept a tight control over the UPA/FNLA activities both within the Congo and without. He provided just enough political and material support to give it international credibility and to provide the Congo with a stake in Angola should the Portuguese eventually leave.[24] The Portuguese, it seems, had little to fear from Roberto and his organisation after the March 1961 attacks.

By the mid-1960s, neither the MPLA nor the UPA/FNLA had met with any substantial success in a classic subversion of the population in the north or in truly displacing the Portuguese position there. This lack of insurgent progress occurred for several reasons. While the army lacked both the manpower and mobility to seal the land border completely in an area of poor roads, dissention between the MPLA and the UPA/FNLA, Léopoldville's favouritism of the UPA/FNLA, and Holden Roberto's failure of leadership served to limit any insurgent offensive. Friction between the two movements had its origins in the external recognition and choice of which one was to be the representative government of any independent Angola. As a consequence, there was intense competition between the two, and this misdirected energy diluted the attention of both in prosecuting the insurgency. Indeed, UPA/FNLA troops took to ambushing MPLA troops in northern Angola, and afterwards Portuguese forces came upon these bloody fratricidal scenes.[25]

Léopoldville's preference for the UPA/FNLA was unabashed, and it worked to give its chosen movement every advantage. As an example, Léopoldville because of its own security problems did not permit insurgents to bear arms within its borders. Both the MPLA and UPA/FNLA insurgents would be transported by Congolese soldiers to the Angolan border, where they would be issued their weapons from depositories. On returning from operations, their weapons would be cantoned, and they would return to their training base with a Congolese escort.[26] Léopoldville employed this control measure to discriminate against and harass the MPLA. In 1962 the MPLA formed its military wing, EPLA (Exército Popular de Libertação de Angola, or Popular Army for the Liberation of Angola), to project its influence into Angola. This nascent force numbered between 250 and 300 young men who had undergone military training in Ghana and Morocco. The EPLA sought to expand the conflict across the northern border of Angola with this force and penetrate the entire country, publicising the MPLA manifesto. Recruiting proved to be difficult because of

Agostinho Neto (left) greeting Fidel Castro (right). (Albert Grandolini Collection)

ethnic rivalries, and military action was thwarted by the competing UPA/FNLA. EPLA troops were often impeded from reaching the border, and their arms confiscated, whereas the UPA/FNLA was accorded privileged and unimpeded access. Despite advantages in the international fora and on the battlefield, Roberto, whose eyes seemed permanently masked behind dark glasses, proved unable to lead effectively in either the political or the military dimension, and Léopoldville sponsorship was unable to reverse this trend.

In June 1963 the UPA/FNLA through its influence with the Congo leadership forced the MPLA to leave Léopoldville and re-establish itself in Brazzaville. Its ability then to project itself militarily into Angola became almost completely circumscribed, and by November it looked more and more isolated. In January 1964 at its Conference of Cadres (Conferência de Quadros) in Brazzaville, it was decided to begin rebuilding the movement as a serious revolutionary force. Part of this plan involved opening a front in the east of Angola through Zambia. The MPLA had made overtures to Kenneth Kaunda, the first president of Zambia following its independence from Britain in 1964. Agostinho Neto, its leader, had also befriended Julius Nyerere, the first president of Tanzania, likewise following its independence from Britain in 1962. These relationships were to prove fortuitous. Beginning in 1965, Tanzania and Zambia permitted the transit of Chinese and Soviet weapons and MPLA cadres across their territories to the eastern Angolan border. Because of this access, the MPLA was able to open a major offensive and to conduct an intensive insurgent campaign in the eastern Angolan districts of Moxico and Cuando Cubango. Preparations were begun accordingly, and by the opening months of 1966 proselytising of the population in the east was evident. The first armed incursions occurred in April, and the war had now clearly moved to the east of Angola. Portuguese resources were redirected to the east and southeast of the territory in response to the new threat.

The Eastern Front

The Eastern Military Zone (Zona Militar Leste or ZML) of Angola was a vast plateau of some 700,000 square kilometres (270,272 square miles) that comprised the districts of Lunda, Moxico, Bié, Cuando Cubango, and portions of Malange and was about seven and a half times the size of continental Portugal.[27] It was a wasteland for insurgent proselytising, as there were only 1.3 million inhabitants in this eastern theatre or about five people per square mile. This latter figure was misleading, as the bulk of the population lived along the CFB or in the primary towns, so in the bush there was actually less than a person per square mile. The goal of the insurgents, of

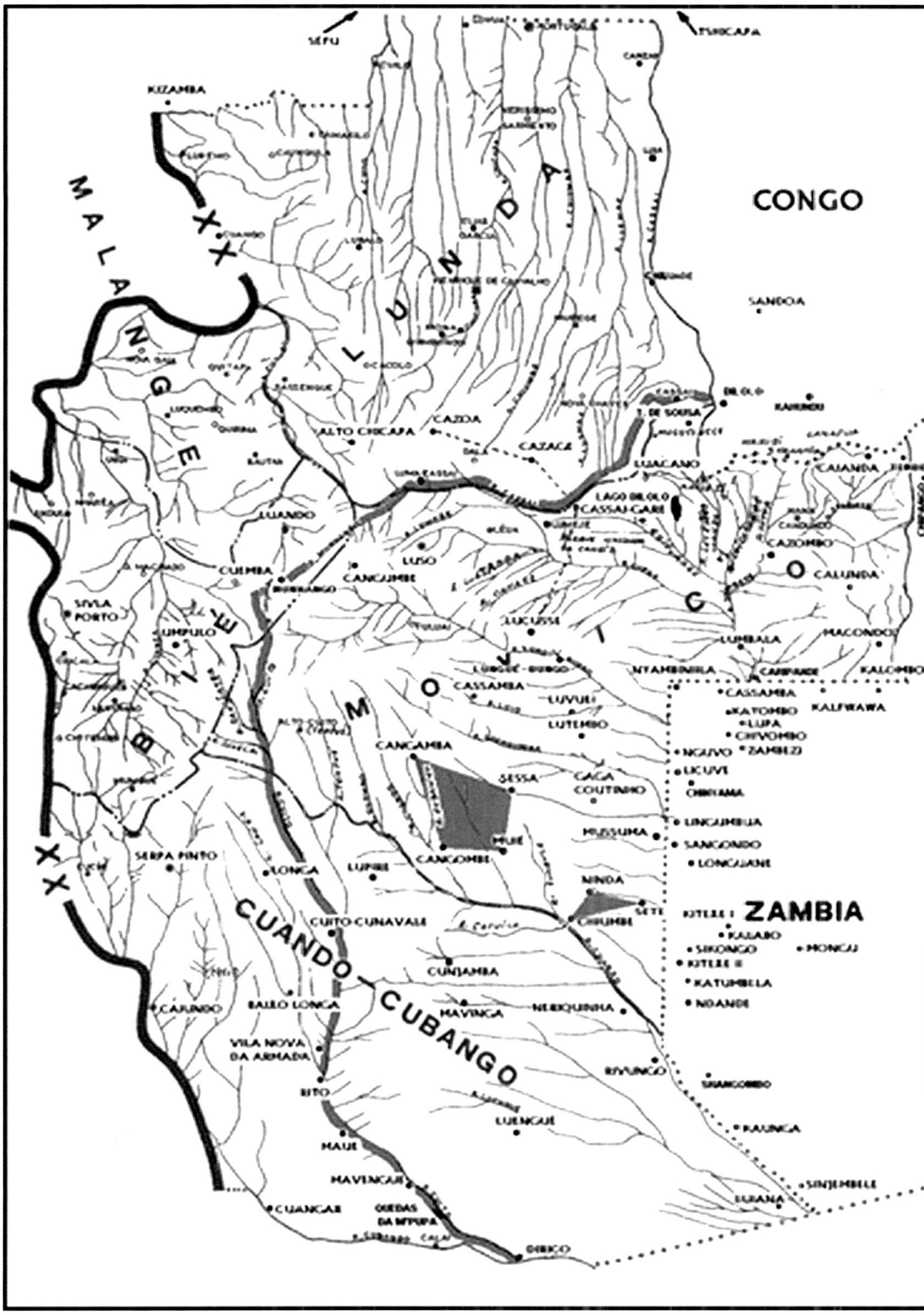

Eastern Military Zone, Angola. (Map by author)

course, was to penetrate far enough westward to where there was a denser population that would respond hopefully to the insurgent message and a significant commercial infrastructure to attack. The problem with this approach was that it was a long and forbidding route to the developed area toward the Atlantic Ocean, and much could go wrong.

This eastern area is a seemingly endless plain with an altitude of about 3,000 feet. Within it there are two elevations, one in Bié and the other in the Cazombo Salient, where the land rises irregularly to about 5,000 feet.[28] The Salient is a square protrusion into Zambia that is about 240 kilometres (144 miles) per side and is divided by the Zambezi River running diagonally through it. On the east side of the river it is mountainous and rocky. To the west of the river it is forested, sometimes densely. It had about 2,000 inhabitants, of which three or four dozen were Europeans.[29]

Overall the ZML was a sprawling savanna sparsely dotted with trees. From the point of view of the insurgent, there were ideal concealment areas scattered through the more elevated lands characterised by ravines and dense forest.[30] Both the vast savannas and mountainous terrain posed significant policing problems for Portugal, for it meant that finding an insurgent column or small "squadron" in either setting was extremely complicated, and gathering the vital intelligence about its activities and intentions was an extraordinary challenge. When insurgent infiltration began in 1966, there were four army battalions in the ZML.[31] At the beginning of 1968 there were six battalions, and by the end of the year there were twelve.[32] Nevertheless, the ZML was a big place and moving even the increased numbers of troops to contact with the enemy and supporting them was difficult.

Insurgent Strategy

The strategy of the nationalist movements was to seek independence for Angola through armed conflict rather than negotiation, although the UNITA strategy was less clear. Accordingly, the MPLA from its Zambian bases planned a two-pronged assault. The southern one would be mounted from Mongu, Shangombo, and Sikongo and known as the Route of the Cuando, as shown on the nearby map that depicts the UPA/FNLA, MPLA, and UNITA external bases and internal military zones. It would follow this river valley westward with the plan of reaching the populated and wealthy district of Bié and the central plain of Huambo, the heart of Angola. From this point the insurgents hoped to control the entire country and to reach all the way to Malange through an axis of advance along the Cuanza River valley.[33]

The northern one was called the Route of the Luena, or the "Agostinho Neto Route" by the MPLA, and was to be launched from Chipango and Cassamba and aimed along this river directly at Luso and from there to the highland plain of Malange. The hope was to gain control of the Luanda-Malange railway, reach Luanda, and link with forces coming from the north.[34] These routes pushing out of the Salient and following the Luena River never successfully penetrated a front defined by an interior line connecting the population centres of Cazoa, Cazage, Cassai-Gare, and Lucusse with Luso as its hub.[35] The MPLA could muster about 4,000 men, of whom about 3,000 were armed. Its operations were centred on anti-vehicle and anti-personnel mines, forced recruiting and intimidation of the population, reaction to Portuguese operations, and some bursts of fire at Portuguese military installations in hit-and-run tactics.[36]

Campaign plans for the UPA/FNLA are much less distinct. Its plan can be imputed from the attempt in 1970 to infiltrate three battalions whose action would bring its forces to the gates of Luanda and precipitate a sudden conclusion to the conflict. By 1971, the UPA/FNLA had approximately 600 men on the eastern front of whom only about 400 were armed. Its offensive was abandoned in September 1972, because its forces were stalemated at the edge of Portuguese territory,

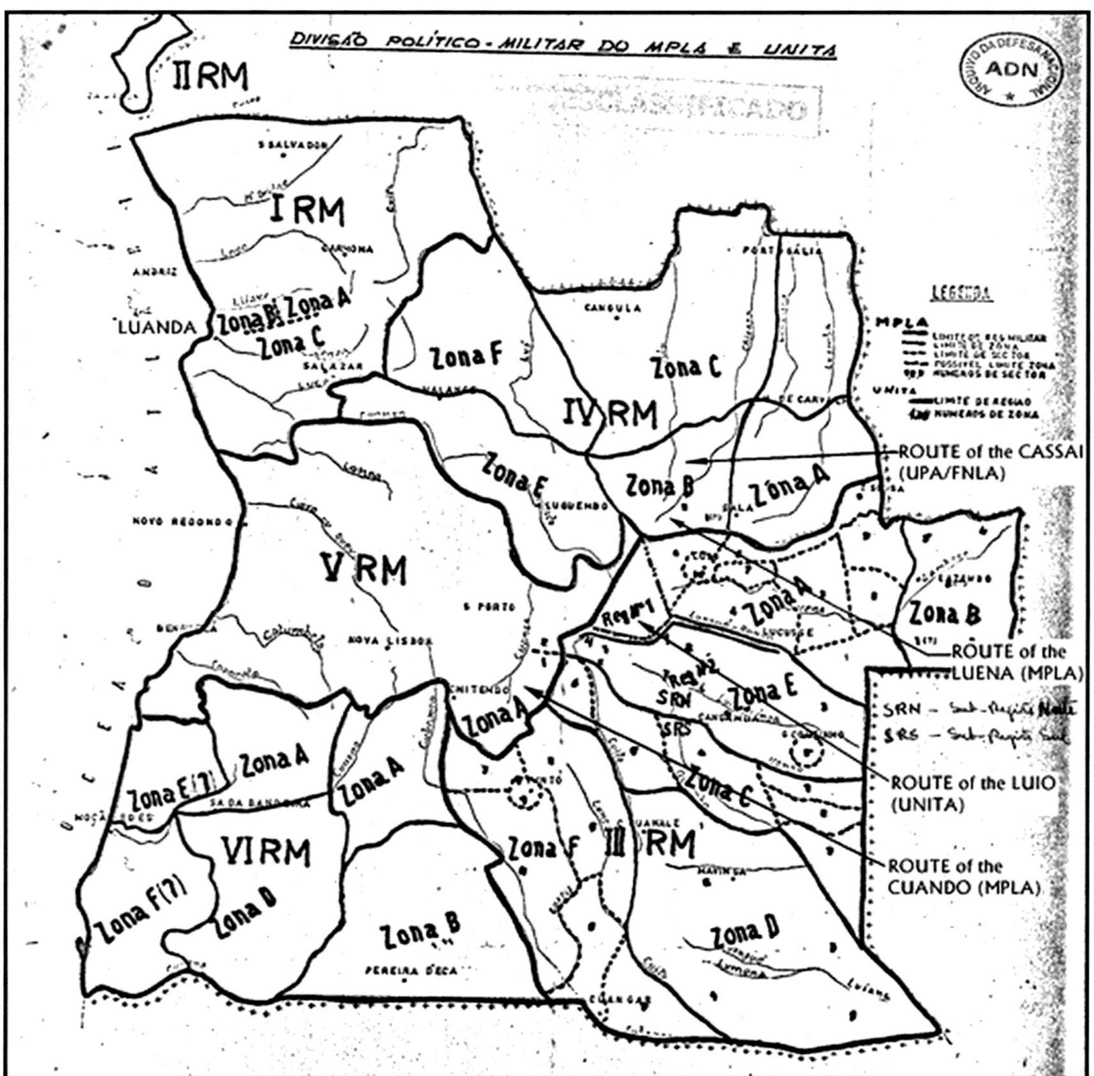

Insurgent routes to the interior of Angola. (Map PIDE/DGS archives as modified by the author)

checked by both the MPLA and the Portuguese in the north and east of the ZML, and thus stood little chance of success. Both UPA/FNLA groups remained relatively inactive as a means of survival.[37]

UNITA simply intended to establish a base deep in the interior of Angola and, using some notion of the oil-spot theory of expanding control, mobilise an ever-increasing number of the population to gain the "total independence of Angola." Indeed, Savimbi was forced by circumstances into this improbable posture, claiming that a true nationalist movement should operate from bases within Angola, as in July 1967 he was finally and completely expelled from Zambia. Certainly, the implementation of such a policy ensured his isolation. By 1971 UNITA was surrounded, and Savimbi counted fewer than 1,300 followers. In order to survive in defeat, he and his men came to an accommodation with the Portuguese. Between 1971 and 1973, UNITA activities were restricted to a prescribed zone at the headwaters of the Lungué-Bungo, and it agreed to cease operations against the Portuguese.[38] As part of this understanding, UNITA would receive arms and medical support and would be free to engage the MPLA.[39] By this time Savimbi had about 500 armed men.[40]

There were substantial weaknesses in the campaign design of all three in that their lines of communication would be long and vulnerable, or in the case of UNITA, non-existent. The goals of each would rely increasingly on the weak strategy of hope, as each moved further and further from its external support and progressively isolated itself deep in the hostile interior of Angola. If these organisations were going to rely on classic proselytising of the population for support, then it would not come willingly. The Angolan people were experiencing new political and economic freedoms and financial prosperity and would hardly welcome what would be tantamount to Napoleonic-type foraging by foreign armies. Then too, the basic premise of all three insurgencies had been removed with successful responses to the people's grievances. Nationalism for the sake of nationalism and the political goal of a single party state running a country for the benefit of its oligarchy or chief-of-state held little popular appeal. Lastly the greatest enemies of the insurgents were each other, as all three were in competition for the spoils to be mined from governing Angola. There was no thought of a coalition government for the greater good of the diverse population.

In contrast, the army in the ZML by December 1971 had about 20,000 personnel, which figure included increasing numbers of commando companies, cavalry squadrons, artillery batteries, engineering companies, a construction company, numerous groups of native auxiliary forces, and a naval and air force presence.[41]

An aerial view of a portion of the Chana de Cameia in eastern Angola during the dry season. During the rainy season the water courses expand, and the chana floods and becomes impassable. Photo Associação de Comandos)

Portuguese Campaign Strategy

In countering this multi-axis assault, the Portuguese were quick to see that UNITA and the UPA/FNLA would be easily contained and that the MPLA represented the real threat. They thus developed a three-phase theatre strategy of first checking the expansion of the insurgent penetration. This would mean defining the population battlefield and bringing security to those threatened. Next, the security forces would surround the insurgents and limit them to a geographic area bounded by the Cuito, Cuanza, Munhango, and Cassai Rivers represented by a by a line running from Dirico in the south to Teixeira de Sousa in the northeast. This was admittedly a substantial tract, but it was thinly populated by any standard and would provide little enemy sustenance. The insurgents could thus do little damage in this isolation and would indeed slowly starve. Within it, Portuguese security forces would relentlessly pursue the enemy, who would become increasingly harried and besieged. Finally, in 1973 and 1974, as the cordon drew progressively tight, the enemy would be completely destroyed.[42]

The need for this lengthy approach was prompted by a number of factors. First, Portugal had limited manpower to police the vast region of the east. This limitation dictated an approach that enlisted the sparse terrain, geographic remoteness, and harsh climate as allies in isolating the insurgents in an attritional war. Second, these three regional characteristics appeared to favour the insurgent in that he could easily hide or move largely unhindered by Portuguese forces, so time was needed to track and destroy him.

The problems of sparse terrain and geographic remoteness were nowhere more evident than in the Chana da Cameia, an extensive plain of some hundreds of square miles completely covered in tall grass. Its extension, vastness, and lack of topographical references made it difficult to navigate and search for the enemy successfully. It was bounded in the north by the CFB and in the south by the Luena River, and the Agostinho Neto Route. In the rainy season it was largely impassable because of flooding, but in the dry season it could be easily crossed on foot, in vehicles, or on horseback. Very few people lived in the Cameia, but the small numbers who did

In the indistinct terrain of the east there were few references, and it was always difficult for the cavalry to match the few that there were depicted on a map with what was observed. Here two dragoons orient the platoon. (Colonel Fernando Luís Franco da Silva Ataide Collection)

were forced to aid the MPLA. MPLA troops in transit through this chana alongside the Luena were difficult to find hiding in the grass and required tailored tactics to weed them out. The proximity of the trackless Cameia to the eastern frontier made it a magnet for insurgent columns trying to elude security forces and move westward.

The weather was another important factor and was indicative of the harsh climate. The rainy season in the east ran from October to March and left enemy columns wet, miserable, and mired. Conversely, it could severely affect Portuguese operations with its electrical activity and towering cumulonimbus clouds. For example, Captain Carlos Acabado, an aviator assigned to commando support, described flying in the east on his way to Sete in the rainy season:

> I saw the airfield in the distance as a trace on the ground, then became preoccupied with the possibility of not having sufficient fuel to circumnavigate the storm that covered the horizon in front of me. Black clouds, so characteristic of the rainy season, rose like high walls from the ground, pregnant with electricity, striking frighteningly, with long and impressionable discharges that appeared immobilised against the dark background, in a spectacularly terrifying but also beautiful force.[43]

This was followed by a dry but cool season characterised by heavy morning fog, the cacimbo, which was caused by the long, cool African nights. Indeed, the transformation from daylight to darkness in the eastern savanna during this period came with such velocity that it was a common sensation that the rotation of the earth accelerated.[44] While this fog hid the insurgents, it invariably hampered operations. Again, Acabado describes one such helicopter commando insertion next to the Quembo River northeast of Cuito Cuanavale during the cacimbo:

> The first section of commandos was launched onto the humid banks of the Quembo, where an intense ground fog persisted. The helicopters touched down and rose in a way that put the men on the ground as rapidly as possible without scattering them. Everything unfolded in a strange atmosphere, blending into a single colour in which sunlight seemed absent and in which the riverbank rose out of the fog … ."[45]

Map reading in the chanas of the east was particularly difficult, as the maps were difficult to reconcile with the actual terrain. Here several officers attempt to interpret the puzzle. (Colonel Manuel Maria Pinheiro da Neves Veloso Collection)

Another difficulty navigating eastern Angola lay in the hundreds of water courses that permeated the Angolan landscape and were deeply affected by the seasons. The extensive riverine network had its origins in the elevations of Bié and Cazombo and made certain that any ground movement by either Portuguese forces or the

In the east of Angola, South Africa saw the territory as a conduit for guerrillas passing from Zambia to Namibia and adopted a policy of helping the Portuguese fight them in Angola before they reached South Africa. Consequently, it began to supply helicopters and aircrews to help. The *Alouette III* helicopters of Portuguese Air Force Squadron 402 were a gift from South Africa, the first five of which arrived in June 1968 at Cuito Cuanavale in C-130 *Hercules* transports in Portuguese livery. These were quickly followed by two more in July and another two in August. Because of their origin, they carried no national identification. It was thought that the casual observer could not differentiate between unmarked Portuguese and unmarked South African *Alouette III*s, both of which operated in the east from this period to the end of the war. Ultimately there were 17 new *Alouette III* helicopters delivered to Angola by South Africa that carried no national markings or serial numbers in order to protect this relationship and the secrecy of Exercise ALCORA, the code name for this military-to-military cooperation. This series became known as the "Black Block" of helicopter serial numbers, because they "did not exist". The *Alouette III* in the illustration is a gift from South Africa and carries only the tactical marking "4" on its side. The primary use of the *Alouette* was the insertion of troops in a surprise envelopment of an enemy position; however, they were used for utilitarian work as well, such as delivering rations for the horses to cavalry platoons on patrol in the remote bush. (Artwork by Tom Cooper)

First corporal
Cavalry Group No. 2
Caserne of Silva Porto
(District of Bié)

By 1970, most Dragoons in Angola were locally recruited, with Europeans only holding the ranks of officers or non-commissioned officers. This first corporal, dressed in ceremonial uniform, wears a variation of the traditional Portuguese camouflage uniform, identified as M/963, which is characterized by pointed flap pockets both in the blouse and trousers. His rank is identified by the bright red chevrons on his shoulder tabs, although in the field the Portuguese wore no identification. As was common among Dragoons, he wears black leather model/967 boots, complemented by long leather gaiters. The traditional "quico" camouflaged headgear is here replaced by a maroon beret, which was normally worn on parade and displays the crossed sabres metal badge of the cavalry. As it is a ceremonial uniform, the Dragoon wears white gloves and only his canvas belt without additional equipment, which appears to be of the American M56 standard or a Portuguese copy of it. His weaponry is the Heckler & Koch G3 7.62mm NATO assault rifle. The model seen here is the most common, with a fixed stock, but the Dragoons also used the retractable stock model.

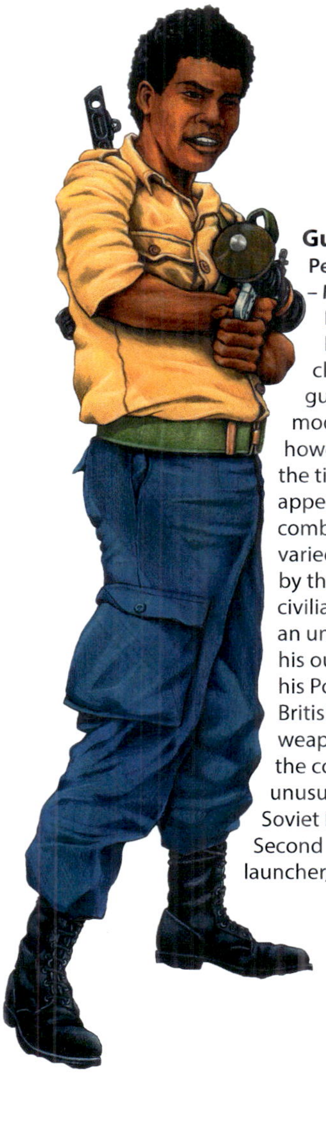

Guerrilla
People's Liberation Movement of Angola – MPLA
Late 1960s

In some early MPLA photographs clearly made for propaganda purposes, guerrillas were pictured dressed in modern combat uniforms and equipment; however, as in any guerrilla force of the time, this was far from the routine appearance of such troops. Guerrilla combat clothing and equipment had very varied origins from the outset, as illustrated by the guerrilla seen here, who wears a civilian shirt and blue military pants of an uncertain origin. The only elements of his outfit that can be easily identified are his Portuguese combat boots and his old British-pattern 1937-style canvas belt. His weapons, as might be expected, come from the communist bloc, and are somewhat unusual in that they combine the outdated Soviet PPSh-41 submachine gun from the Second World War and a modern RPG-7 rocket launcher, a frontline infantry support weapon.

Captain
Cavalry Group No. 1
Caserne of Silva Porto (District of Bié)
Easily recognized by the three yellow stripes on the shoulder tabs, this Dragoon captain wears the standard attire for this type of troop, namely camouflaged M/964 uniform, long-legged cavalry boots and the traditional "quico" camouflaged headgear. On his canvas belt he has a leather holster containing his Walther P38 pistol and a set of bags similar to those used at the time by the West German Army. His primary weapon is a Portuguese version of the standard German-made Heckler & Koch G3 7.62mm NATO assault rifle, which was most likely manufactured in Lisbon under license by the Fábrica de Braço de Prata and known as the G-3 assault rifle. Horse rations and supplies were just as important as the Dragoon's combat arms and in this case the horse feed bag is visible. The tack is the M/938 standard harness and the M/42 saddle, complemented by a leather rifle sheath, field blanket, tent, 3P campaign bag, and a camouflage tarp. For a patrol there would be additionally large bags of feed attached to the saddle.

A patrol moving through the Chana de Cameia.

A patrol pausing for a rest in the Chana de Cameia. Dragoons would begin their patrols at a walk for perhaps 30 minutes, then trot for about the same time, and then canter for perhaps 20 minutes before repeating the sequence. After 2 hours, the platoon would rest.

A platoon on patrol would often travel in columns of two – when there was a road available. However, if they were near a suspected enemy area, then there was always a possibility that the road would be mined.

Finding water in the Chana de Chameia was a difficult issue during the dry season. Here two dragoons have located a rare spring and are watering their horses.

Portuguese Angola
1960-1975
Cabinda
San Salvador
(M'banza Congo)
N'zeto
Ambriz
Uige
Caxito
Luanda
Luremo
Camxila
Cafunfo
Malanje
Henrique de Carvalho
(Saurimo)
Calulo
Mussende
Teixeira De Sousa
(Luau)
Porto Amboim
Gabela
Novo Redondo
(Sumbe)
Luso
(Luena)
Cazombo
Cela
Lobito
Silva Porto
(Kuito)
Benguela
Novoa Lisboa
Cangamba
Capelongo
Menongue
Cago Coutinho
(Lumbala)
Mocamedes
(Namibe)
Sa de Bandeira
(Lubango)
Cassinga
Techamutete
Cuito Cuanavale
Caiundo
Mavinga
Chiange
Porto Alexandre
(Tombua)
Luenge
Baia dos Tigre
Pereira D'Eca
(Ongiva)

Dragoons in the rainy season. Everyone alike was wet and miserable. (Colonel Manuel Urbano Moreira Dias Collection)

Dragoons crossing a water course in a chana. The approaches and stream bed were often soft to the point of a horse sinking completely with rider and equipment in attempting to cross. Here the dragoons dismount and carefully lead their mounts safely across. (Colonel António Vital Fernandes Faia Collection)

enemy would involve one or more river crossings. Some were easily fordable and others extremely difficult, depending on the season and what the rains had done. Portuguese troops exceled in negotiating this extensive river system. They developed the skills to cross any river, day or night, and to use it as a natural obstacle to enemy manoeuvre and as ideal defensive terrain. The rivers proved to be avenues of enemy approach for combat and lines of communication for enemy infiltrations. These latter characteristics were to help in predicting the location and routes of enemy incursions. Rivers also served as natural boundaries to the battlefield and provided navigation references and orientation.

Because of the nature of the battlefield and the enemy, a containment and attrition strategy was well suited and logical. It was one in which Portuguese forces would define and then gradually reduce the area of insurgent contamination, and the enemy would be forced to fight from a progressively circumscribed and isolated position and be ultimately eliminated. The few local people living in the east and southeast could hardly subsist themselves, much less support the insurgents with food, recruits, intelligence, and shelter. In summary, Portuguese theatre strategy was based on sound reasoning that followed from a considered appraisal of opponent strengths, battlefield terrain, resident population, and available Portuguese resources.[46]

While the military dimension was important in this strategy, it had to be integrated with and built around the notion that the war in the east was a fight to preserve and protect the population from insurgent intimidation. This meant organising it to defend itself and supporting it in every way with such skills as medical care, animal husbandry, and education. The job of the military was to suppress violence and provide a security umbrella under which Portugal could earn the loyalty of the population. This way of fighting required extensive coordination across civil-military tasks as much as military ones.

Acabado recounts an event illustrative of the Portuguese effort to secure this loyalty during one of the many actions in Operation Siroco. A commando group was launched in a surprise vertical envelopment at dawn on a zone where it was known that the enemy was present and could only survive with the help of the population or with the knowledge of the local tribal chief. The raid was considered a great success and produced insurgent losses, captured arms, and valuable documents. The village of the tribal chief and other local settlements were located adjacent to the insurgent encampments, so obviously the people knew of the enemy, yet neither the chief nor his people were molested by the commandos by order of their commander.

The next day at dawn four jeeps transported the commander and six of his commandos, all unarmed, to the primary village to pay a courtesy call on the chief. He was surprised at the visit and wondered

A close link with the sparse population in the chanas was important in supporting it. Here a platoon of dragoons pause at a village in the Chana de Cameia to visit with its people and gather intelligence. (Colonel Manuel Urbano Moreira Dias Collection)

to his men how important this meeting with the chief had been. The maintenance of trust in relations with the population was important both for the people as well as the Portuguese troops. In the conduct of war, it was important to be generous with the weak, who cannot always be protected, as they should be. The duty was upon the strong to practice good manners and not intimidate the population.[47]

Opening Moves

Subversion of the population in the east of Angola was estimated at 6 percent in 1965 and had steadily risen from that figure to 42 percent in 1968, when the MPLA offensive reached its height.[48] In 1966, Portugal was heavily occupied with the northern front, as while the

General Francisco da Costa Gomes. (Albert Grandolini Collection)

Brigadier José M. Bethencourt Rodrigues. (Albert Grandolini Collection)

about the motives of the commander, who explained what his commandos were doing and that they would be in the area for some additional days. In turn the chief told of the insurgents coming to his village, where the people were unarmed and defenceless, and of his inability to inform the authorities. Later the chief came to the commando encampment to bring some goats and chickens which he laid at the feet of the commander in a very African ritual. The chief was given a chair next to the commander, smoked a cigarette, drank some beer, and finished with a glass of brandy. Finally, he thanked the commander emotionally for taking care to avoid his men, women, and children in the assault. Much later the commander explained

MPLA and UNITA in the east were making their initial forays, there remained a substantial threat from the north that required attention. The north remained a priority until the completion of Operation Flank Attack (Golpe de Flanco) in late February 1971, which finally neutralised the UPA/FNLA there.

War in the east had begun in earnest in November and December 1966, when some MPLA insurgents penetrated the northeast corner of the Cazombo Salient near the border settlements of Jimbe and Caianda. UNITA also entered the fray, and Savimbi's first attack occurred in December 1966 on the post of Cassamba. He made another two weeks later on Christmas Eve, when 500 UNITA insurgents attacked the Portuguese garrison of Teixeira de Sousa and suffered a disastrous defeat with 234 dead. UNITA and the MPLA were soon alienated from their vital patron, as Portugal struck at the fragile Zambian treasury by closing the CFB to copper exports for a week. Again, in April 1967, there were two UNITA acts of sabotage on the CFB infrastructure, and again Portugal closed the railway and threatened lengthier closures unless attacks ceased. Thereafter UNITA was unwelcome in Zambia, and the MPLA likewise was put on notice not to interfere with the CFB.

Portuguese leverage had its roots in Zambian dependence on the CFB to export its copper ore across Angola. The railway always represented a tempting target for insurgents, and thus Zambia found itself caught between the practical need for foreign sales and the ideological desire to support nationalist movements. CFB closures carried a strong message for both Zambia and the Congo. As a consequence, during early 1967 the MPLA was ostensibly pushed out of Zambia and infiltrated the east in two primary areas, Lake Dilolo on the western edge of the Salient, and a larger area located about 160 miles due south of Luso and bounded by the settlements of Sessa, Muié, Cangombe, and Cangamba. By 1968 this surge had penetrated as far west as Bié district, and as a result of such overextension, various MPLA columns found themselves quite vulnerable. Considerable numbers were destroyed or captured, but by 1970 there were still 1,300 men in Zambian bases supporting regular columns into Angola, a constant threat.[49] Clearly there were limits to diplomatic and economic pressure in the face of Kaunda's strong feelings about African nationalist movements

When General Francisco da Costa Gomes arrived in Luanda in May 1970 as the new Commander-in-Chief, in the midst of this enemy offensive, he began by reorganising his headquarters staff and establishing an Office of Irregular Troops, which coordinated the specialised African troops, various militias, and other irregular forces. These troops, including the cavalry, with their unique tracking skills and familiarity with the local terrain did much to locate the enemy columns in the vastness of eastern Angola. Costa Gomes also shifted focus to the east in March 1971 and selected Brigadier José Manuel Bethencourt Rodrigues as the ZML commander. He was granted wide latitude in executing the containment and attrition strategy, and as we shall see, was completely successful in this effort.

3
ENTER THE HORSE

As troops began operating in the Angolan environment after the March 1961 attacks, they experienced a series of problems and began to search for solutions to them. One such suggestion was made by Captain António Ferrand d'Almeida in a 1963 article in the journal *Revista da Cavalaria* that Portuguese forces employ horse cavalry in Angola. He expanded on some of the needed considerations in bringing horses to the battlefield, such as adaptation of the horse to local conditions, its feeding, logistics, and operational usefulness.[1] On the last issue, he talked about cavalry being able to maintain "permanent contact with the indigenous population," an important and needed characteristic of government troops in a counterinsurgency. At the time, however, the fighting was in the mountainous north of the territory, and the insurgents had sought internal sanctuary deep in the Dembos, a rugged area of dense tropical forest. Using cavalry to engage them in such restricted terrain was clearly impractical because of their vulnerability to tropical disease and other weaknesses, still the seed was planted. José Talhadas, a fuzileiro who operated there, describes conditions:

> I was in the Dembos where I learned that a prolonged silence in the bush was an indication that there were others present, the scene of an ambush, that a cry in the night carried dozens of kilometres, that any negligence ended human survival, and that any laxness could result in the death of the comrade in front or behind me.[2]

Indeed, the Dembos was a place of deep shadows, luxuriant vegetation, dense forest, tall trees, and surprisingly uneven terrain with elevated and rocky hills, and all of this was accompanied by an overwhelming humidity that made everyone sweat profusely. Tropical rainstorms routinely added to the discomfort. Talhadas describes his camouflage battle-dress jacket as being perpetually soaked, as if he had just washed it.[3] Clearly using the horse in this environment was a somewhat impractical proposal; however, the fight was moving to more accommodative terrain, so the appeal gained momentum. Portugal was, after all, engaged in an asymmetrical war and was attempting to adapt, so the notion might have merit and be worthy of consideration.

Ferrand d'Almeida followed with another forceful article in 1964 making the case for horse cavalry in Angola as a solution to some of the developing mobility problems and under certain conditions more effective than motorised troops.[4] In 1965, Lieutenant Colonel Luís Barros e Cunha followed with an article, also in *Revista da Cavalaria*, on likely horse cavalry missions.[5] This author's approach was more technical and defended the usefulness of horse cavalry, an idea that might extend to selected areas of both Angola and Mozambique. He suggested looking at history for some lessons, as we have done. The notion of using horse cavalry units to fight counterinsurgency, however, differed from their use in the Chana de Mufilo or at Macantene in that it would not be the quickness and discipline of the charge that would carry the day. Instead it would be the flexibility and ability of the force to adapt to the terrain and successfully conquer an invisible enemy.

The following article in the same issue by Major Joaquim Miguel Duarte Silva continues this theme with a deeper study and reminds the reader of the successful military expeditions to Angola and Mozambique in the late nineteenth and early twentieth centuries and the advantages of horse cavalry units to them. He worried that use of the horse was not addressed in the new Portuguese doctrine for subversive war and that this omission might doom its consideration. Yet there was nothing in the doctrine that precluded imaginative thinking, and perhaps he was unaware that the U.S. Marine Corps in its Small Wars Manual devotes an entire chapter to "Animal Transportation," so the idea was certainly neither obsolete nor discarded by other nations considering counterinsurgency despite the general move to mechanisation.[5] Still there were

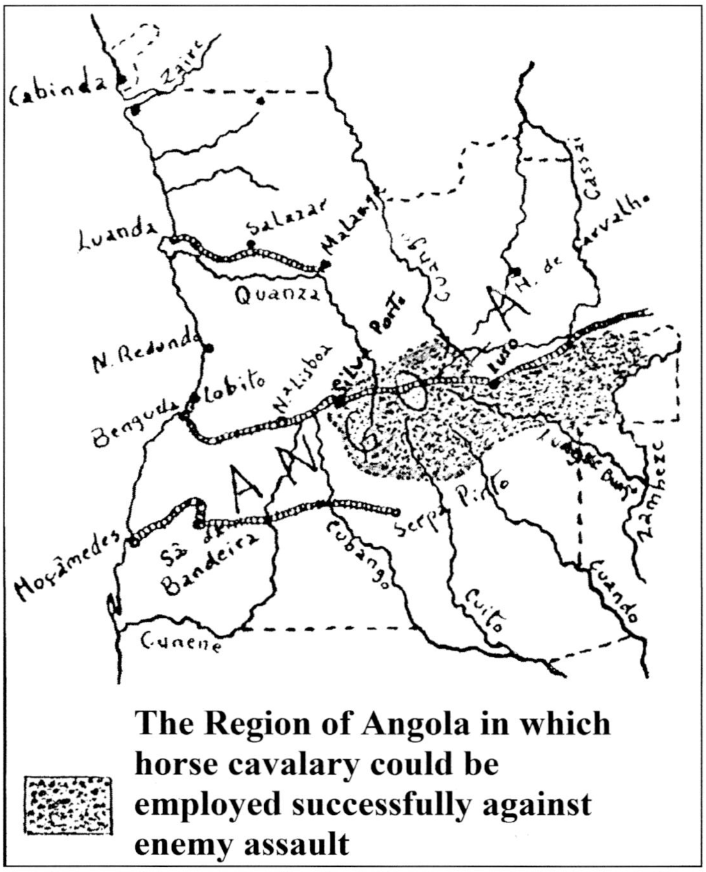

Cavalry operating area extending from Silva Porto to the Cazumbo Salient. (Resenha Histórico-Militar das Campanhas de África 1961–1974, 6th Volume, Tome I: Angola–Book 2, p. 321)

Experimental cavalry platoon on parade during its development. (Colonel Manuel Maria Pinheiro da Neves Veloso Collection)

naysayers who thought the horse and its rider in the field would offer a large and vulnerable target for insurgent fire and would present costly problems with their health needs and requirements for special instruction and shelter.[7]

These expressed opinions were not without influence, and in January 1966, when MPLA elements clearly were beginning operations in the east of Angola from their Zambian sanctuary, and the likely operating area would lend itself to cavalry operations, the Subsecretary of State for the Army visited Angola. He was briefed about the possibility of establishing a pilot program with a platoon-sized cavalry unit to explore the feasibility of the concept.[8] Accordingly in September of the same year he verbally authorized a sum of 200 contos (200,000$00 escudos or about $7,000 at the time) to purchase horses from the Republic of South Africa to initiate the trial. This was considered a bargain, as it cost less to purchase the required thirty horses for the platoon than it cost for a Berliet truck.[9] Yet it was the Commander of the Military Region of Angola (Região Militar de Angola or RMA), General Manuel Avelino Barreira Antunes, who saw the potential of the project and supported it despite his manpower and budgetary constraints. He soon foresaw the need for a full squadron of horse cavalry, and as we shall see, he got a bit ahead of events.

In January 1967, a subaltern of cavalry, Alferes Manuel Neves Veloso, was appointed specifically to command the new experimental platoon, which was to be organised along traditional lines and located at the base in Silva Porto (today Cuíto), the capital of Bié, a province of eastern Angola. He arrived there from the metrópole in mid-March and reported to Cavalry Group No. 1, a mechanised unit to which the horse platoon would be attached. It might be well to mention that the new mechanised cavalry was poorly adapted to operating in Angola and countering the insurgency there. Captain Luís Manuel Silveira Vicente da Silva in a 1971 article in *Revista da Cavalaria* detailed this failure and entered the long line of those advocating a return to the tailored use of horse cavalry in eastern Angola.[10] Status of the platoon was such that it was not considered part of the order of battle in Angola, as its only mission was to conduct the experiment.[11] Yet UNITA had attacked the post at Cassamba in December 1966, so the experiment was being conducted when the operational need had been identified. Still the Vice Chief of Army Staff, General Sá Viana Rebelo, held the position that the platoon should not be considered as a reinforcing unit until its final report was completed. This was confirmed by the Minister of the Army, General Joaquim da Luz Cunha.[12]

During its year in existence the experimental platoon had to test everything: The equipment; the fodder and supplements, as there was a lack of minerals in the water; the most useful way to instruct and train the new horses and men; and even the construction of stables.[13] The adaptation of horse cavalry to modern guerrilla warfare necessitated a substantial revision and rewriting of earlier, traditional regulations and tactical procedures. The new guidelines would be specific to eastern Angola and to a sole cavalry group there, so while it would be innovative, it would not be new institutionalised doctrine.

Silva Porto was the obvious choice, as it was located on the CFB and was at the edge of the proposed cavalry operating area.[14] This positioning would allow the platoon to be logistically supported by rail and to experiment at the western edge of the area well away from potential enemy contact while gaining the needed knowledge. Later cavalry units would be deployed to other forward locations, also on or near the CFB rail line but nearer the traditional enemy penetration routes following the Luena ("Agostinho Neto Route") and the Lungué Bungo Rivers directly toward Luso (today Luena) and their headwaters. These moves were important to the developing campaign in the east, for they supplemented the increasingly lengthy transit routes and made for a shorter ride on horseback to engage the invading enemy. As he was driven south and eastward into Zambia and reduced, transit by train and columns of trucks over tarred roads to preposition the horses, as from Silva Porto to Serpa Pinto in the south, to areas further eastward and the establishment of forward operating bases, such as Munhango, would be used to avoid exhausting them in transit to their operating areas.[15] While the selection of Silva Porto represented sound strategic positioning, there was a sound tactical one as well.

The soil composition in Angola varies from clay in the northern regions to soft, sandy soils in the south and southeast and was well-studied. The best terrain for horses is the softest possible, largely free of stones and pebbles, as it allows the horses to be ridden without horseshoes – a great logistical advantage. The most propitious operating area with this type of softness was located in the vast extended plains that ran to the east and south of Silva Porto and hence its appeal. Even with the soft soil, the experimental platoon and each platoon thereafter would be assigned a farrier, as while the horses had hard, durable hooves, and the terrain few stones, he was regularly needed to keep the hooves trimmed to balance the horse's foot and stride. Corrective trimming was also occasionally needed to improve the stride or gait of the horse.

Forest cover in Angola also varies with the thick forests in the northern Cabinda and Dembos, to medium vegetation in the middle, and finally to light cover in the south. Horse units are affected by this cover, as it should be thin enough to allow reasonable mobility while at the same time thick enough to provide adequate concealment. A Portuguese Army study of the Angolan terrain reached the conclusion that horse cavalry units would fare best on the central plain with its combination of soft soil and medium cover.[16]

Equipment and Arms

By the time of the experimental platoon in late 1967 Portuguese soldiers in Angola were wearing a camouflage battle dress, and this was customary with the new cavalry. The standard arm was 7.62mm G-3 assault rifle, a copy of the Bundeswehr G-3 manufactured under license in Portugal. It was at first carried across the saddle, but this position proved cumbersome. Later a scabbard was added that could be mounted either under the left saddle flap or on the rear of the saddle. In either case it could be extracted and ready in seconds. In early actions the rifle was used both from the horse and on foot; however, it proved somewhat cumbersome, and the Walther P-38 pistol was later favoured for greater practicality and responsiveness, particularly from horseback. Generally, it was carried drawn when enemy contact was anticipated, and in the case of an ambush and charge at the enemy, it could be fired at a full gallop, although as a defensive weapon and not with any particular accuracy.[17]

The saddle was the traditional cavalry or

Horses being unloaded from a CFB car and prepared for an operation after having been transported by train to their operating area further eastward from Silva Porto. (Colonel Manuel Maria Pinheiro da Neves Veloso Collection)

Interior of a CFB horse car showing horses being loaded. (Colonel Manuel Urbano Moreira Dias Collection)

Horses being transported by train to their operating area further eastward in preparation for an operation. (Colonel Vasco Luís Pereira Esteves Ramires Collection)

Horses being loaded onto a CFB car for the trip home to Silva Porto following an operation. (Colonel Vasco Luís Pereira Esteves Ramires Collection)

Horses being transported in a contract conveyance to their operating area further east of Silva Porto. (Colonel António Vital Fernandes Faia Collection)

Horses being transported in a Berliet truck to their operating area further east of Silva Porto. (Colonel Manuel Urbano Moreira Dias Collection)

military saddle with an array of D-rings around it for attaching bags of feed, bedding, and weapons. It had a breastplate to prevent the saddle slipping to the rear of the horse during vigorous manoeuvres. A double bridle was favoured with snaffle and curb reins.

Feed and Medical

The health problems for both the horses and men that had been the scourge of earlier campaigns in Africa were practically eliminated through prophylactic care and vaccinations that modern medical and veterinary science permitted.[18] The initial remounts came from South Africa, as it was convenient, but still there were a number of adjustments required to acclimate the horses to their new environment. Inoculation, diet, and sanitation were in the forefront.[19]

Vaccinations against horse sickness, blackleg, and tetanus, medication for piroplasmosis and worms were all administered regularly. Coupled with these medications were simple hygienic practices, such as prophylactic treatments with a bath, whether arriving as a new remount, that is, an unbroken new "recruit" horse, returning from field operations, or following instructional outings in the bush.[20] Likewise vitamin food supplements and mineral salts were administered daily to reduce the chance of sickness, as the horses were always vulnerable in the stable environment and under heavy exercise conditions. Indeed, at the conclusion of each operation it was normal for both men and horses to exhibit signs of deep fatigue, and most horses would have lost weight – in some cases as much as fifty kilogrammes.[21] In their weakened state the horses always needed careful attention. The stable floor was disinfected weekly and the stable generally on a similar basis.[22]

Daily feeding consisted of six kilogrammes of a mixture of 1.5 kilogrammes of local forage, 3.0 kilogrammes of ground corn, and 1.5 kilogrammes of oats – administered in 2.0 kilogramme portions three times a day.[23] In the field the typical operation lasted between four to five days, so each horse would carry his own rations of 18.0 to 22.5 kilogrammes of this feed mixture packed in individual plastic sacks for each feeding.[24] The plastic protected the feed from the humidity. Later these capabilities were extended, as the horses attained excellent physical conditioning. Patrols could then be conducted between eight and twenty-seven days in length with periodic resupply by helicopter or truck about every five days without difficulty.[25] A patrol of eight days would typically cover about 250 kilometres and would extend further with increased duration.[26] For the experimental platoon the longest-ever recorded distance covered operationally was 420 kilometres.[27] On patrol the normal speeds were the walk at six kilometres per hour, the trot at twelve kilometres per hour, and the gallop

Dragoon with his rifle in a forward scabbard in later operations. Th s proved ideal. (Colonel António Vital Fernandes Faia Collection)

A Dragoon with his G-3 7.62mm assault rifle athwart his saddle as in early operations. This carrying method proved awkward and was changed constantly in search of an easier method. (Colonel António Vital Fernandes Faia Collection)

Dragoon officer with pistol holster containing his Walther P-38 9mm readily available on his right hip. Note his hand signal, as the dragoons silently move through the bush. (Colonel Manuel Urbano Moreira Dias Collection)

A Dragoon with his rifle strapped to the right front side of the saddle. This proved better than carrying it athwart loosely, but the dragoons had not yet found the ideal. (Colonel António Vital Fernandes Faia Collection)

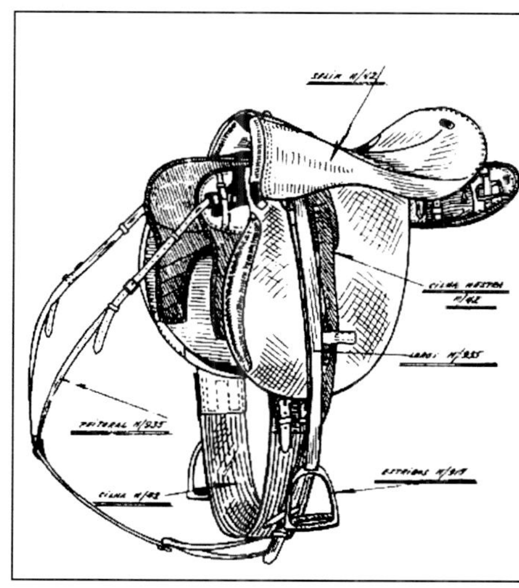

Military saddle as used by the dragoons with its breastplate shown to the right. (Arquivo Histórico Militar)

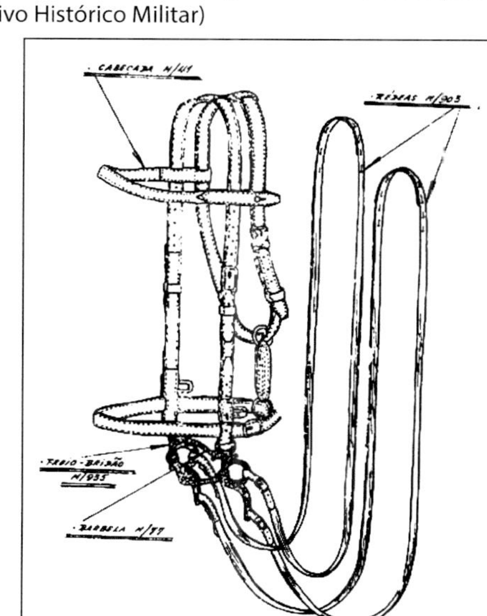

Double bridle displaying the snaffle and curb bit reins. (Arquivo Histórico Militar)

Dragoons washing their horses while the grooms disinfected the stables in the absence of the horses. (Colonel Manuel Urbano Moreira Dias Collection)

Dragoons join their mounts in a routine bath as a part of regular equine hygiene. (Colonel Fernando Luís Franco da Silva Ataíde Collection)

Horse being fed in the field on an operation. Note the ventilation holes in the bag to aid in breathing. (Colonel António Vital Fernandes Faia Collection)

at eighteen kilometres per hour. It was normal to trot for fifteen minutes and then walk the horse for five minutes of rest.[28] This rhythm allowed an average speed of advance of eight to thirteen kilometres per hour or about fifty kilometres a day when patrolling, which was many times that of a man on foot.[29] In case of necessity each day could be increased to sixty or even seventy kilometres for three days. In extraordinary circumstances a horse could cover one hundred kilometres in a single day but on the preceding and following days must not exceed fifty kilometres.[30] This achievement was not without careful adjustment to the operating conditions in eastern Angola and the help of a team of veterinarians from both Portugal and South Africa.

Obtaining water in the central plains of Angola was rarely a problem on operations; however, it became increasingly important during the dry season, as the usual sources could be surprisingly empty. In one instance during an operation in the region of Fort Cameia, south of Lumeje, it was necessary to lead the horses for two days, resting in the shade during daylight and travelling at night, until the platoon arrived at the Luena River for watering.[31] Generally a horse can go a day without water and three days without food before collapsing.

Mixing the horses from the remounts with those already in Silva Porto inevitably invited trouble, as the new arrivals frequently brought infections with them that spread, particularly if they had travelled exposed to the weather. Under such conditions there were cases of hyperthermia as well as other possibilities. This vulnerability

A closer look at the feed bag in operation. The ventilation holes are clearly visible. (Colonel António Vital Fernandes Faia Collection)

Resupply helicopter in a landing zone marked by smoke flares. (Colone Fernando Luís Franco da Silva Ataíde Collection)

Radio contact with a resupply helicopter for a platoon on an extended patrol. (Colonel Manuel Urbano Moreira Dias Collection)

Argentinne remounts in transit from Argentina to Lobito, Angola. (Colonel António Vital Fernandes Faia Collection)

A mounted dragoon monitoring an Alouette helicopter that brought the supplies to the unit deployed in the bush. (Photo by Fernando Farinha)

Stable with the straw pile prior to the fire at Silva Porto. (Colonel António Vital Fernandes Faia Collection)

Aftermath of the disastrous fire at Silva Porto in which forty-three horses perished. (Colonel António Vital Fernandes Faia Collection)

An injured horse that had to be put down in the field. Injuries were infrequent, so it was a sad day when a horse was lost. (Colonel António Vital Fernandes Faia Collection)

Sometimes in the vastness of the chana a platoon would encounter a bridge across a water course over which the horses could be led with relative safety, but this was rare. (Colonel António Vital Fernandes Faia Collection)

Horse flounders in the soft mud bank of a water course in a chana. (Colonel Fernando Luís Franco da Silva Ataíde Collection)

The two dragoons quickly move to remove his load and lead the horse to safety. (Colonel Fernando Luís Franco da Silva Ataíde Collection)

This horse crossing a water course suddenly sank completely. The dragoon on the left is holding the horse's head above water, while the dragoon on the right is freeing the horse of his load. (Colonel António Vital Fernandes Faia Collection)

With additional help the horse is worked to firm ground and escapes the mud. (Colonel António Vital Fernandes Faia Collection)

Dragoon feeding his horse hay. Note halter laid over bridle with lead coiled and secured alongside horse's head. This arrangement allowed for both a rapid access to a lead in case of need and an easy method for carrying it at the ready. (Colonel Manuel Maria Pinheiro da Neves Veloso Collection)

was solved by isolating the new mounts and stabilising them with veterinary care, until they were again healthy and acclimated.[32] As they recovered individually from their voyage, they were integrated into the stable. Probably the most severe cases occurred with an early remount from Argentina in which sixteen horses died from an epidemic of strangles. After this incident it was policy to isolate all arriving remounts until they could be safely integrated with the existing horses.[33] Horses in southern Africa were an irregular breed, as the natural fodder and water lacked the proper vitamins and minerals. They were prone to sickness and lacked durability. After the initial remounts from South Africa, purchases were made from Argentina, which produced magnificent horses. These were solid stock and both less expensive and better adapted to the climate than those of South Africa.[34]

Yet with all of this conscientious care, there were the accidents, and in this case the disastrous straw fire at the end of 1973, in which forty-three horses were destroyed in a receiving stable, was the most notable.[35] In the instance of the fire, it is thought that the electrical installation short-circuited and set the straw aflame. Unfortunately, the newly-arrived horses were inside, and in less than three minutes from the beginning of the fire until the collapse of the building the courageous service personnel ran inside the inferno heedless of the consequences to save forty-seven horses.[36]

Horses rarely died from enemy gunfire, and through 1973 there had been only seven such deaths. Various others had been wounded on the average of one every four months in Angola, but in the majority of cases they recovered fully.[37]

In addition to these losses, there were additional occasions of unanticipated sickness and accidents. Naturally there were some fractured limbs from the strenuous activity of operations that required putting down the horse. There were three cases in which a horse died from the bite of a venomous cobra, and another two horses succumbed when swarmed by wild bees when they disturbed a hive while drinking next to a river.[38] There were also cases of internal lesions resulting in a madness in which the horse threw himself on the ground and rolled around in an attempt to seek relief.[39]

One of the trickier manoeuvres during operations in the field was a stream crossing in the chanas. As mentioned, the soil in this region was soft, and the chanas were cut by water courses that required crossing. Often the banks of these courses and the bed of the streams were soft to the point of being quicksand. A platoon making a crossing always searched for one with solid and firm ground that would support a horse safely. Still mistakes were made, and these could result in the enormous work of extracting a horse who had sunk to his head in mud. If the crossing was likely to prove difficult, then the tack was removed to lighten him and allow him to deal with the mud, and he was carefully helped across. In the event of his sinking, the troopers had about twenty minutes to extract him before he gave up, dropped his head, and died. While few horses were lost in this way, it nevertheless posed a serious risk and was an ever-present danger.[40]

Cavalry tended to operate in vast tracts of wilderness where there were few roads and even fewer passable ones during the rainy season. Hence the enemy was unable to anticipate the route or timing of patrols, so encountering mines was thus an infrequent event. When a horse did step on a mine, he was inevitably killed, although the rider generally survived.[41]

Horse being led across a dangerous water course after being lightened. White horses were not favoured, as their colour highlighted them in a combat environment, and they were readily visible to the enemy. (Colonel Fernando Luís Franco da Silva Ataíde Collection)

Two dragoons of local recruitment on patrol in eastern Angola. (Calvert Collection, Liddell Hart Centre for Military Archives)

Ferrand d'Almeida describes a number of other incidents. Once on an operation, his platoon encountered a family of lions consisting of a male, three females, and their cubs. All began to utter threatening roars and feigned charges at the platoon, always stopping at a respectful distance. The platoon continued on its way, and it was curious that the Argentinian horses all maintained an unperturbed calm despite the intimidating actions of the lions and the apparent danger from the strange animals.[42]

Another interesting case recounted by Ferrand d'Almeida was of a horse, also Argentinian, that stumbled and fell with its rider during pursuit at a gallop across an anhara — a large extension of creeping grass found in the upland regions of Angola along the margins of rivers — in an attempt to catch a small group of enemies sighted in the distance. The horse got up and continued to run without his rider and was soon hidden by the tall elephant grass. There was a fruitless search for his tracks the next day by a light aircraft. After little more than a month, a combat group of flechas, specialised native troops who worked for the police and normally operated in this area, sighted the missing horse in the midst of a herd of palancas, very large antelopes native to the Angolan savannah. Because of the impossibility of recovering him alive, they shot him

A column of dragoons in the bush. Note the vantage point from horseback over the vegetation. This gave the dragoons a clear advantage over an enemy on foot and the ability to follow paths and trails through the foliage. (Colonel Manuel Urbano Moreira Dias Collection)

in the hope of recovering his tack, which he was still wearing, but it was so deteriorated from exposure to the weather that it was not worth the effort.[43]

Ferrand d'Almeida's last story on animal health was about the stable dog named Nero, whose behaviour when a horse was sick was one of the great unexplained mysteries to all. Nero was a large dog, an ill-defined mutt, who seemed to know so as well. He was always appearing punctually for the more serious daily activities around the barracks and stables and in the field. Over time he developed a keen awareness of the horses among whom he lived. When a horse was taken ill and likely to die, Nero would stay with the horse, lying beneath his manger and only leaving for short periods to eat. Ferrand d'Almeida notes that the unit had never seen a dog comfort horses in this way – supporting an animal who was gravely ill in its struggle to recuperate. Sadly, the presence of Nero at the head of the sick was always a sign of certain death. Nero, however, could not predict his own death. One day, in the course of an operation, he was destroyed by an enemy booby trap.[44]

Recruitment and Training

Because of a long-standing mythical notion that it was almost impossible to train natives for cavalry service or that it would take a prolonged training period to educate them for such service, recruitment was initially conducted within army units located in the metrópole.[45] However, it was found that there were few potential recruits with experience in riding a horse, so recruits were sought through volunteers already serving in Angola. This served the purpose of the small experimental unit, which was short-lived and for its participants an obvious success even before the test was concluded. However, in future units, with the exception of officers and sergeants, cavalry troops tended to be recruited locally from indigenous soldiers who were serving their two-year compulsory military service. Prior to 1796 it was forbidden to import mares into Angola for fear that the Angolans would develop cavalry units of their own to challenge the Portuguese. Consequently, there were few horses in Angola, and early recruits were unlikely ever to have seen one let alone have a working experience with one.[46] This made it difficult to adapt to what was for them a strange animal. Hence the recruiting effort was directed toward a certain native people in the southwest of Angola, the Cuanhamas and the Cuamatos, who were very fierce and had a long experience in raising cattle. As they were familiar with large animals, they adapted easily and quickly to the horse and proved to be excellent riders.[47] While it is difficult to say precisely what percentage of the recruits were indigenous, in one squadron all of the troopers were Cuanhamas or Cuamatos with the exception of one European, two mestiços, and a black.[48]

Indeed, there developed an affectionate relationship between these native dragoons and their horses despite the fact that they had not previously been a part of their culture or habitat. Horses were treated as a fellow brother-in-arms for whom the dragoons would take great care and exhibit heartfelt concern. There were many examples of this attachment, and in one case when a young soldier was wounded in action, his first thought was of his horse. Once assured that the horse was uninjured, he asked that it only be ridden by his commander while he recovered.[49]

Training a trooper required three months to make him combat ready. The initial six weeks consisted of basic military training and riding lessons.[50] The second six weeks were dedicated to the "binomial man-horse," that is, learning to work with the horse and becoming a functioning team. The last week featured an 80–100-kilometre battle course to test and improve the trooper's skills in the field with his mount and to confront him with all of the key situations that he might encounter on the battlefield.[51] This training in Silva Porto was reminiscent of that at the Practical School of Cavalry last conducted at Torres Novas with adaptations to the African environment. In 1970 a centre for instruction was established at Silva Porto, and over 300 mounted troops

Recruits learning to ride. (Colonel Fernando Luís Franco da Silva Ataíde Collection)

A recruit learning to take obstacles on horseback. (Colonel Fernando Luís Franco da Silva Ataíde Collection)

Recruits moving in company across the natural obstacle of a roadway. (Colonel Fernando Luís Franco da Silva Ataíde Collection)

Recruits learning to jump their mounts. (Colonel Manuel Maria Pinheiro da Neves Veloso Collection)

A recruit mastering the art of riding over rough terrain. (Colonel António Vital Fernandes Faia Collection)

were trained there in the basics of equitation and cavalry tactics during the war.[52]

Just as at Torres Vedras, the day began with the recruits learning to care for their horses. The first task was to clean a horse's stall and replace the bed with fresh straw. Then preparing for a march, the recruits would learn the proper inspection of the hooves and the tack and its adjustment. On the march after twenty minutes, it was appropriate to pause to adjust the bridle, the saddle girth, and the equipment. At the end of two hours a small stop of ten minutes was needed both to rest the horse's back and to permit the men to satisfy some necessities. For a march of several days, some days were begun by leading the horse for two or three kilometres before mounting. This would clear his kidneys and bowels and stretch his muscles before the rigours of a long ride. During long overnight stops, the horses had their saddles, bridles, and equipment removed and were cleaned, watered, and fed. The cleaning involved a minute inspection of the horse for possible problems, a thorough brushing, and finally a smoothing of the horse's hide with a cloth.[53]

The recruits also learned how to load horses in railcars. The horses were assembled adjacent to the station and loaded in a trailing line with a spacing of three metres. Once aboard, the horse was led to its position in an organised, sequential, and quiet way, all being positioned facing the aisle. It generally took one-and-a-half railcars to transport a platoon, and a trooper was assigned to ride in each car to look after the mounts with smoking strictly forbidden.[54]

The report on the platoon was completed at the end of 1967, and its most important conclusions were that horses could easily adapt to the climate in the central plains and the south of Angola; a mounted unit was more useful than an infantry unit; a horse cavalry unit was less expensive and more reliable to operate than an equivalent mechanised one; and employment of horse cavalry units produced great psychological benefits.[55] While sceptics argued that the horse would present a large target to an enemy, be vulnerable in a firefight, and represent yet another mouth to feed and animal to train, in tests it was found that horses were a confusing target and difficult to hit when charging head-on. In firefights horses were rarely wounded, as the enemy was not usually prepared to stand in the face of a charging horse with its rider firing. It was not only psychologically intimidating to the enemy but was dangerous for him. Experience was to support these tests.[56] The report further noted that experimentation with the platoon had always been made in the bush to test its adaptability and capabilities in the realism of the field. As a result, many traditional cavalry practices and tactics were found still to be valid and adopted with needed adjustments to accommodate conditions in Angola.

Prior to 1969 cavalry operations were conducted as a single force of platoon strength. Always the platoon deployed in the bush, avoiding the paths and trails that wound across it. Its deployment was generally in two sections in a line abreast that presented a front no less than 300 metres across and a third section trailing. From the end of 1969 cavalry operations expanded to squadron strength and began to be integrated and coordinated with other units operating in the sector, as resources were being shifted at this time to the east to address the growing insurgent assault. With the increase from platoon to squadron strength units, additional formations came into use.[57]

Recruits learning to negotiate a river bank on horseback under the watchful eye of an instructor. (Colonel António Vital Fernandes Faia Collection)

The river claims a few recruits as they take a spill in this exercise. (Colonel António Vital Fernandes Faia Collection)

The most popular and effective basic tactical organisation in tests was the platoon deployment made with three sections of thirteen mounted troopers each plus a support section of one machine gunner, three rifle grenadiers, an orderly, a bugler, and a farrier.[58] This was deployed in a number of formations in the field. A popular one diagrammed nearby was the T-formation. This was formed with two sections in line abreast with the commander in the centre providing a front of some 200 to 500 metres, depending on the density of the vegetation.[59] This formation provided the most effective sweep of the terrain while maintaining the proper line of sight for hand signal communications and commands from the commander in his central position. This line abreast was backed by a third section as a reserve positioned in column formation trailing the centre. The design provided excellent manoeuvre options when contact was made with the enemy and in the two-hour rotation of the sections that allowed the trailing section to relax.[60]

Another popular one was the double echelon or wedge formation, which was also between 200 and 500 metres wide. This could be quickly changed to a single echelon or a line abreast or a ranked formation, depending on the terrain or tactical situation.[61] Alternatively there was the L-formation, which could be quickly changed into a line or column.[62] The underlying notion behind each of these was to maintain a large enough front to protect against ambush. It was very difficult for insurgents to ambush a patrol, as they were on foot and unable to see the horsemen well enough through the tall elephant grass for surprise. The mounted troops could see over the vegetation and undergrowth and identify insurgents readily from this vantage. Normally the terrain cover was such that an enemy guerrilla had a field of fire of only about 30 meters, while that of the mounted trooper was about 50 metres. Also, the cavalry line of advance was some 300 metres wide. Should an ambush be attempted, the formation would execute a wheeling movement toward the attack and surround the insurgents, as shown

Recruits ride their mounts through parked helicopters with blades turning as part of an acclimation process with the aircraft. (Colonel Vasco Luís Pereira Esteves Ramires Collection)

View of a cavalry platoon practicing its deployment in a T-Formation in the field. (Colonel Manuel Urbano Moreira Dias Collection)

One wing of a seasoned cavalry platoon deployed in a T-Formation in the field and moving at speed. (Major General João Gilberto de Mascarenhas de Sousa Soares da Mota Collection)

in the accompanying diagram. With the advantage of speed and height, the cavalry prevented the normal shoot and scoot tactics of the guerrilla, and enemy encirclement and capture or destruction in such instances was almost certain.

On patrol these formations allowed for an enormous flexibility in addressing enemy moves and were practiced by each platoon beforehand until they were thoroughly understood. When challenged by the enemy in some way, the dragoons reacted instinctively at the danger and the signal of the commander, for procedures ultimately had to be learned and ingrained behaviour to be executed correctly under the pressure of combat. Whether it was executing something simple, such as establishing security for watering the horses from a stream or protecting a campsite, or something more complicated, such as crossing the danger of a water course with soft banks or an anhara, it was always a familiar procedure. For immediate action, it was always a question of surprise. Whether it was the enemy or the dragoons being surprised, the objective regardless of the circumstances was always to annihilate the enemy. There were several variables associated with enemy contact that dictated dragoon action. The first was the time of day, and the second was the nature of the terrain, open or covered. The third was the relative direction of the enemy, and the last was his strength. To the practised dragoon, these would be processed immediately, and he would move with his platoon as one, understanding what was needed and his role in it.

Aside from the usual moves on horseback to envelope the enemy force when contact was made, there were some interesting mixed mounted and dismounted approaches that bear viewing in more detail. One of the more difficult

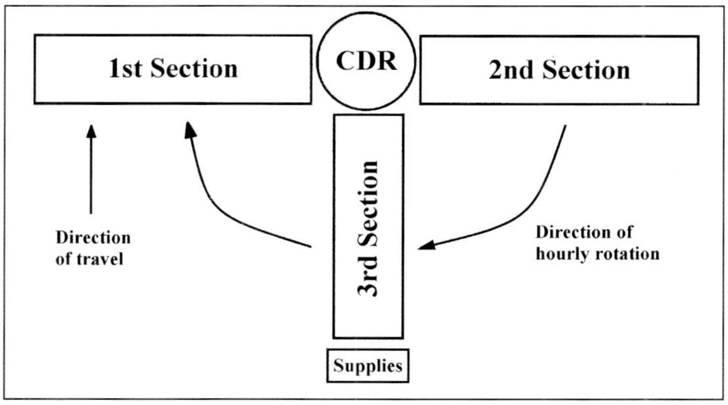

Plan view of a deployed cavalry platoon showing the orientation of its three sections and the direction of relief rotation. (Drawing by the author)

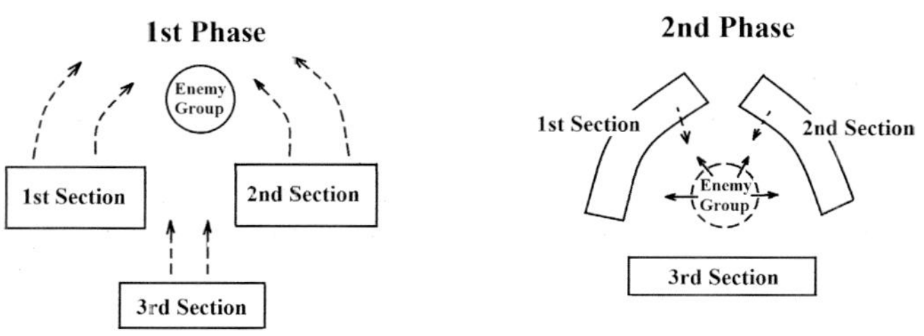

Plan view of a deployed cavalry platoon showing the moves by each section to address an enemy group, to contain it, and prevent its fleeing. In this case the enemy group is straight ahead; however, if contact is made on either the left or right flank, then that contacting section becomes the blocking force and the other two sections move to envelope the enemy. (Drawing by the author)

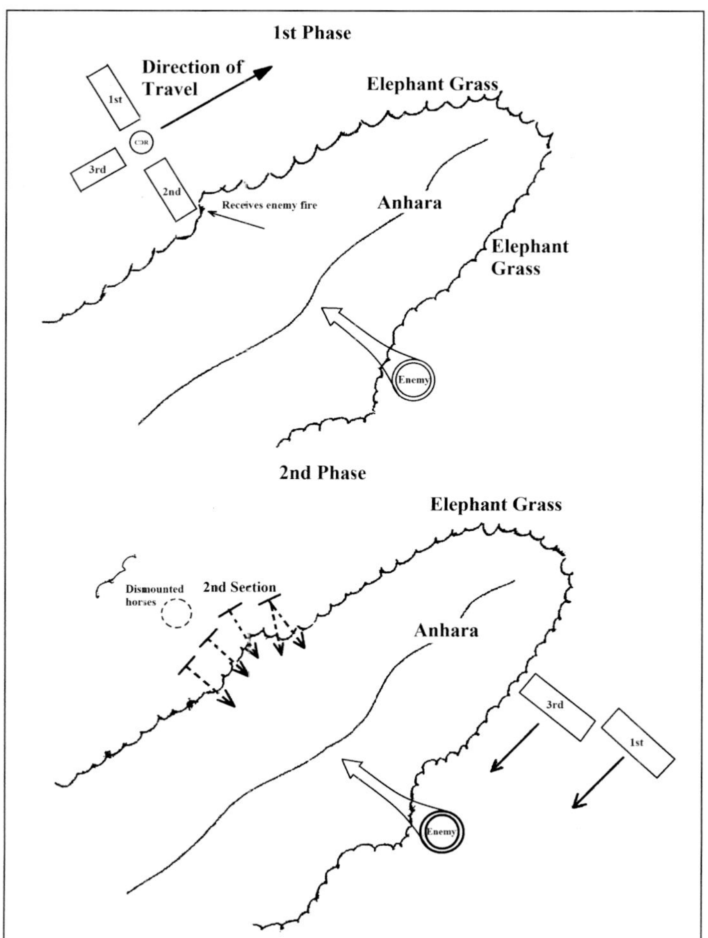

Plan view of a deployed cavalry platoon on patrol taking fire from across an anhara and its subsequent action. (Drawing by the author)

Charging dragoons chase down an ambushing insurgent. (Major-General João Gilberto de Mascarenhas de Sousa Soares da Mota Collection)

Another view of charging dragoons catching an insurgent. (Colonel Manuel Urbano Moreira Dias Collection)

situations occurred when there were bursts of enemy fire against Portuguese cavalry on the move. It was especially difficult when the enemy positioned himself behind an obstacle that was difficult to cross, such as a marshy anhara. In these conditions the enemy sought to insulate himself from the advantage of the horse and against any other danger and yet in firing draw Portuguese troops to the anhara in the hope that they would try to cross and become easy targets in the mire. In such cases, the section or sections taking fire immediately dismounted, dispersed, and returned fire. This would fix the enemy. The remainder of the force moved at speed to find a way to skirt the obstacle and outflank the enemy. Often these enemy groups numbered as many as thirty armed guerrillas.

In one particular example, shown in an accompanying diagram, the enemy force, in anticipation of the approach of a cavalry platoon, established itself behind an anhara with the idea of firing on the platoon as it passed next to the anhara on its far side. Hopefully this fire would draw the horses and riders into the morass of tangled vines and grass, where they would become immobilised and vulnerable to attack by foot soldiers. Reaction of the platoon was not as expected by the enemy. The 2nd Section, receiving the enemy fire, dismounted and dispersed, and began to return fire. Meanwhile the 1st and 3rd Sections skirted the anhara and attacked the enemy flank, destroying the force.

If the force believed that it was being followed by guerrillas, then it was split into two platoons, with one travelling a few kilometres behind the other. The first would patrol normally and aim to attract the guerrillas, while the other would aim to catch the guerrillas following the lead platoon by surprise.[63]

Later three platoons would comprise a squadron, and three squadrons a group.[64] Initially sections were comprised of three-man squads – one man to hold the three horses and the other two acting as an infantry team. Later the basic concept was changed to a six-man

Dragoon guarding horses. (Armando Monteiro Collection)

squad with one man holding horses and the remaining five acting as infantry. This organisation was flexible and was mission dependent. For instance, if the platoon needed to dismount distant from its objective, then additional men would remain with the horses.[65]

Meanwhile in October 1967, while the experiment was incomplete, yet an obvious success before its conclusion, Barreira Atunes acted. The RMA proposed to the army staff the idea of moving immediately to establish a full squadron of cavalry.[66] The army waffled on the idea, and soon Viana Rebelo found himself having to justify the reluctant army position to the Minister of Defence. The army wished to wait for the experiment to be completed, as there were significant teething problems. Recruiting and obtaining instructors for the experiment had been difficult.[67] An immediate expansion from a platoon of thirty men to an operational squadron of 150 created additional pressure on both the instruction and recruiting weaknesses, as an expanded instruction program would be needed to create this new capacity.[68] Manpower would have to come from existing RMA units, all of which were undermanned.[69] Undoubtedly the increased noise level both officially and unofficially with a steady drumbeat of articles, briefings, and memorandums in favour of standing up a cavalry squadron had had a marked effect. The proposal of a tactical level adaptation of horse cavalry was embraced by the operational commander and had the endorsement and support of the strategic leadership. This personal commitment and support throughout the chain of command ensured that the required resources were available as they were needed when the squadron was established.

Cavalry Group No. 1

In 1968 at the conclusion of the successful experimental platoon, the RMA established a three-squadron cavalry group (Grupo de Cavalaria No. 1) at Silva Porto, which was commonly called the dragoons of Angola (Dragões de Angola). The term dragões, which was unofficial but widely used, indicated that the troopers were in fact mounted infantry. Indeed, in forming the group, the RMA did not immediately have enough horses to mount the entire force. As a consequence, one of the squadrons formed was an independent cavalry company of light infantry organised into four combat groups or platoons. After a year of fighting as such, the company received its mounts and was reorganised as a true cavalry squadron.

The concept of operations for this new and expanded force was to explore the areas little frequented, contact the population, collect intelligence, and capture or destroy enemy elements identified. Typically, missions centred on patrolling and post-attack sweep operations. For instance, once a column or group of insurgents was detected breaching the border and making its way into Portuguese territory, arrangements were generally made to gather intelligence on its numbers, composition, direction, and speed of travel. Gradually it was isolated and attacked by a helicopter assault with paratroopers or commandos, although other ground troops, such as flechas, could be used. While this original assault generally destroyed the force as a significant threat, there were invariably those who escaped and hid, and these represented a continuing menace. These strays would continue to prey on the local population and otherwise remain a danger to territorial security, hence they required capturing or dispatching. This task was one for the dragoons who would sweep the area of engagement looking for signs of stragglers, engaging the local population, destroying insurgent infrastructure, uncovering weapons and food caches, and policing isolated areas.

One of the more typical of these operations was the combined arms of Operation Strong Wind (Operação Éolo) conducted between 8 August and 1 September 1971. Its purpose was to destroy an identified insurgent camp, as an enemy group normally would penetrate the frontier with Zambia and travel several days into Portuguese territory before pausing to rest and regroup. It was at this point that it generally built huts for shelter and established a base that could support further penetration westward. Sometimes a base was simply a temporary rest stop of a westward-bound group and would be abandoned after a short period. In other cases, a base was more permanent and served as part of an intended support

Cavalry Group No. 1 on parade. The commander with the bugler and standard bearer are in front of the squadron formation. (Colonel Fernando Luís Franco da Silva Ataíde Collection)

Dragoons engaging with local villagers during a patrol. (Colonel Vasco Luís Pereira Esteves Ramires Collection)

Dragoons interrogating an enemy prisoner captured during a sweep operation. (Colonel Manuel Urbano Moreira Dias Collection)

infrastructure for additional columns or groups in transit. These sites generally contained food and weapons caches. In either case, the RMA sought the destruction of these enemy groups and their infrastructure.

In this particular instance, two platoons of dragoons operated in support of a heliborne paratrooper or "para" assault to reduce the enemy. The area of operation was divided into two sectors, and each force was assigned its own sector to separate the two forces, as the operation was planned in two stages. The sector designated for the

Dragoons holding an enemy prisoner for questioning. (Colonel Manuel Urbano Moreira Dias Collection)

helo assault contained the targeted enemy base, and while the attack was underway, it was designated a "hot" or "red" status. Such an airborne operation would last at most a few hours. Meanwhile, the dragoons waited in the adjacent sector, until the paras concluded their phase of the operation, and the "red" sector was designated "green". At this point the dragoons were to enter the former para sector and begin their sweep and pursuit of those enemy who had escaped. This two-phased approach was aimed, first, at the surprise and shock of an airborne assault, as any ground approach would be protracted and the enemy might escape, and second, the longer-term pursuit of enemy elements who may have escaped.

As the tropical dawn approached at the para base on the morning of the operation, the Alouette III helicopters were ready with their blades turning in a constant rhythm. The paras, fully briefed and prepared, ran to the waiting aircraft with their bodies bent and heads lowered to avoid the blades above. With all aboard, the helos lifted off in sequence, each creating an enormous swirl of dust. Once airborne, the paras in the half-light scrutinised the horizon through the curved windshield in search of life in the immense savanna ahead of them. For more than an hour the helos flew over scrub trees that dotted the inhospitable expanse, when at last they spotted a small copse of trees – the target. The helos approached the edge of this wood to hover and deposit the paras. By all indications this isolated copse was the correct choice, as it provided the only opportunity for concealment on the endless horizon of the chana.[70]

When the paras jumped the one-metre distance to the ground in disembarking and began to run as one, the force split into two teams side by side and partially surrounded the wood. It was difficult

Dragoons burn the huts of an abandoned enemy encampment in the east of Angola. (Colonel Manuel Maria Pinheiro da Neves Veloso Collection)

Dragoons discover and burn an abandoned enemy hut discovered in the east of Angola. (Colonel Vasco Luís Pereira Esteves Ramires Collection)

Weapons captured by the dragoons during a raid on an enemy base in the east of Angola. (Colonel António Vital Fernandes Faia Collection)

to see its interior, but as the paras advanced, they encountered a group of small huts well hidden in the dense thicket. The first team opened fire on some guerrillas who were caught by surprise and fled in various directions. The team, well trained and disciplined, pursued the enemy to the middle of the camp and investigated hut after hut with an elevated proficiency and professionalism. The enemy, now in flight, returned fire wildly. The team on the southern flank wounded two and killed another insurgent. The team on the northern flank encountered some resistance and forced the enemy to flee into the fire of the other team, killing two more insurgents.[71]

The landing had been well organised and brilliantly executed as dawn broke. It completely surprised the enemy and denied him adequate reaction time. By every indication he was still in bed sleeping, tired after a long march with a heavy pack across the

Rest day during a patrol. (Colonel Vasco Luís Pereira Esteves Ramires Collection)

Dragoons pause for a meal during the rest day of a patrol. (Colonel Manuel Urbano Moreira Dias Collection)

sandy ground of eastern Angola. Fortunately, the paras suffered no mishaps. When it was over, the paras shared their relief and joy in the midst of the miniscule encampment of six huts that were little more than low shelters. The complete surprise of the enemy was the clear reason for success. The insurgents who escaped had a long road to safety with few places to hide and would not likely survive for long with the dragoons in pursuit.[72]

For the dragoons, their move into the paras' now "green" sector began the patient and lengthy work of securing the area and pursuing the escaped enemy eastward. The cavalry operation lasted thirty-five days, and the cycle for the two-platoon squadron during this time was one day of rest for every five days of operations. The squadron could advance about fifty kilometres on a good day, if there were no interruptions, and would over the course of the operation ride some 560 kilometres.[73] Resupply occurred on each rest day and was done by a combination of helicopter and truck.[74] The difficulty of the operation cannot be exaggerated. In riding this distance across the seemingly infinite savanna, with heat, thirst, danger, and the tension of combat as constant companions, both horses and men became extremely fatigued. The constant demands of the animals and the need for an elevated number of rations – four or five daily – were additional factors. Under these conditions only troops profoundly disciplined and determined could survive and function. Yet the dragoons' enthusiasm for the mission and their dedication to it animated them during all that followed and reflected a deep esprit de corps. Physically this was a demanding operation, and in the end both horses and men lost significant weight. Despite the difficulty of the operation and the hardships imposed on man and beast, the few of the enemy who escaped the paras remained at large.

Similarly, a few months later in February 1972, Operation Exult (Operação Exultar) covered some 800 kilometres through bush in thirty-four days in the area between the Bala and Cuvelai Rivers with the aim of destroying the MPLA presence there. This location was designated by the enemy as his Sector 6, Zone C, III Military Region (Região Militar or RM) and was situated on his Route of the Cuando, one of the popular MPLA avenues for penetrating Angola from the southeast.[75] The area was located about 90 miles due south of Munhango. The operation resulted in the destruction of six enemy bases, the capture of diverse weapons, and the liberation of about eighty elements of the population under enemy control.[76] The policing of this remote and inaccessible area was made possible by the appreciable tactical mobility of horse cavalry that was able to locate and follow the trails left by the enemy.[77]

This enemy III RM extended across the entire MPLA front between Zambia and Angola and encompassed the Angolan districts of Lunda, Malange, Bié, and Cuando Cubango. It was under direction of the MPLA commander Iko Carreira, who oversaw the two primary routes of infiltration, the Route of the Luena and the Route of the Cuando, both of which largely followed the rivers of the same names. His comments in a report on the formidable horse cavalry are worth quoting:

> We are fighting the whites, but today came the war with the horses. They killed many here in the area between the Chifumage and Luena Rivers. We five here waited for me to inquire first to the subsector of Kakeya, but when word from Kakeya came, it was to tell us to flee. When we are afraid, we normally go there. First… there is nothing that can go against the cavalrymen, no comrade can run with the horse, as running with the horse attracts fire. Here in the chanas, even if comrades are sent to fight the horses, they will not be successful. The soldiers, when they are mounted and fire at us, make it difficult, and there are many of us who have died. We do not know when the president will visit, but perhaps when he comes he will make us withdraw. We do not know, but we remember that while we are still alive, we can flee.[78]

Such an enemy appraisal of the effectiveness of horse cavalry in the fight against the MPLA in the vast and open savannas of the east of Angola says much about the effectiveness of the dragoons. This is deserved, as the dragoons lived up fully to the expectations envisioned at their creation, and the Commander of the Eastern Military Zone, General Bethencourt Rodrigues, counted on them for the execution of consequential missions consistent with their operational capabilities. These were invariably performed with brilliance and achieved excellent results.[79]

Looking Back

War in the east had benefitted from the earlier learning period between 1961 and 1969 in addressing the enemy in the north. During the opening enemy moves in the east, specific task forces were assembled to address a targeted incursion and threat. The overall strategy remained directed to the north, until proselytization of the eastern population arose alarmingly in 1968. When the east required attention and resources, it received them. Bethencourt Rodrigues proceeded by defining the battlefield and developing a strategy of containment and attrition to address the vast open spaces of the east and the limited Portuguese forces. Integral to his solution was the use of highly mobile elite hunter-killer forces and the dragoons. Air support was the key in this campaign and its success.

Wounded evacuation by horse to the point where a helicopter can land for a medical airlift. (Colonel Vasco Luís Pereira Esteves Ramires Collection)

Wounded being loaded into an Alouette III helicopter for medical evacuation from the field. (Colonel António Vital Fernandes Faia Collection)

Bethencourt Rodrigues understood precisely the intentions of the enemy and easily predicted his behaviour. Costa Gomes was able to release the needed resources to the east. By April 1974, the UPA/FNLA and the MPLA were destroyed. For the UPA/FNLA the crisis was complete. For the MPLA, it was reduced to sneaking across the border from its bases in Zambia and planting mines along the frontier roads. Its actions along the border were violent and short in both duration and penetration. The notion here was to strike a blow against the Portuguese that would open the way for a column to penetrate inland. This never worked.

In the observation of Carlos Acabado, all of the military superiority that Portugal ultimately enjoyed in the ZML was the result of the arrival of Bethencourt Rodrigues. His warfighting methods transformed the theatre of operations. There was a profound revolution in the strategic and tactical concepts, and for the first time in the history of subversive war, the guerrilla was conquered. More importantly, however, was the mobilisation of the population, with funding support, to effect an economic recovery that led to indispensable social stabilisation.[80]

In an appraisal of the situation by Brigadier Hélio Felgas, Bethencourt Rodrigues's relief, he reported that by the beginning of April 1974 there was no contact between Portuguese forces and the insurgent groups of any of the nationalist organisations. By the end of April, the southeast of Angola was calm and insurgent activity was practically non-existent.[81]

In an interview with the journalist José Freire Antunes following the war, Daniel Chipenda of the MPLA had this to say about the effectiveness of Portuguese strategy:

> From 1972 we faced a crisis in expanding, because we had lost the capability to control a major part of the population that had retreated from the frontier. Conversely the Portuguese army, with its psychological action, succeeded in controlling the strategic villages where the population was administered by the army. This was a difficult phase between 1969 and 1972. We felt that this Portuguese offensive was a very real one. It was a phase of great difficulty. We could not deliver on the promises of a better way of life for the population, as an incentive in the struggle against the Portuguese administration. And the population that we were able to affect was united, more or less, in understanding this.[82]

The population sought to escape control of the MPLA and the other nationalist movements and nowhere was this more evident than in the explosion of education during the war in Angola.[83] By the 1970s under the protection of the security umbrella one saw daily thousands of children in their white smocks walking to school. The undisputed statistics prove this learning expansion. A decade previously such a phenomena would have been hard to imagine.[84]

4
THE THREAT TO MOZAMBIQUE

Mozambique probably would not have become a war theatre but for the independence of Tanzania in 1961. It was the emergence of Julius Nyerere, first as its premier and later in 1962 as its president, that was the most telling development, as he was an ardent nationalist who was passionately committed to supporting and providing a home for African liberation movements. These included the African National Congress (ANC) and the Pan African Congress (PAC) of South Africa, Zimbabwe African National Union (ZANU) and Robert Mugabe in their struggle to unseat the white regime in Southern Rhodesia (now Zimbabwe), and most importantly to our story, Front for the Liberation of Mozambique (Frente de Libertação de Moçambique or FRELIMO).

Nyerere was a generous host to FRELIMO and provided the ideal sanctuary from which to project power into northern Mozambique. Unfortunately, FRELIMO needed much more than a refuge to be successful, as both geography and internal conflict conspired to make its insurgency difficult. Mozambique is about 1,800 kilometres in length, and FRELIMO forces had to travel about half that distance through barren and hostile territory to reach significant numbers of people to proselytise. This they were never able to do.

Eduardo Mondlane, who with Nyerere's help had consolidated most of the disparate Mozambican nationalist movements into FRELIMO, was personally endorsed by him as its leader in September 1962.[1] Nyerere had selected him to lead FRELIMO while he was teaching anthropology at Syracuse University and brought him to Dar-es-Salaam, because he had not been involved in any of the earlier, bitter disputes between the several nationalist organisations resident in Tanzania. It was thought that this credential would make Mondlane a less polarising and more capable peacemaker.

FRELIMO had begun with a planned program of infiltration, subversion, and intimidation of the population, and raids against Portuguese infrastructure. There was the hope of mass insurrection against the Portuguese authorities, again in the vein of Holden Roberto's logic, but the population was too sparse, dispersed, and divided for this course to be a realistic expectation. Until 1967, FRELIMO was not able to extend its activities beyond the border districts of Cabo Delgado and Niassa. Its insurgent incursions were limited to penetrating the territory short distances with small groups that made attacks. These were actually strikes in that they normally originated from bases in Tanzania just across the border, and after a brief hit-and-run action in Mozambique, the attackers quickly returned to their sanctuary.[2] There were some elements of FRELIMO who lived among the population in Cabo Delgado, and these provided intelligence and assistance.

When this strategy failure became evident in the late 1960s, FRELIMO reorganised itself at its 2nd Party Congress held in July 1968 at the settlement of Matchedje in a "liberated zone" in north-western Niassa. The site was a few miles into Portuguese territory from the Tanzanian frontier in very remote and sparsely populated terrain and was only "liberated" in the sense that for the five days of the Congress the attendees went undisturbed. Its reorganisation consisted of merging its civil and military components and establishing a military force within Mozambique organised by sectors, each with its own battalion formed with three companies of 150 men each. The regular forces were to be supported by a popular militia. This was the ideal; however, 450 men in a battalion at a FRELIMO base would quickly attract Portuguese attention, so in practice it was modified to fit the battlefield.[3]

In 1968 FRELIMO acted to initiate a second front in the Téte District prompted by Zambian permission to do so.[4] In looking at a map of the area, one can readily see that it would have been far easier to use Malawi for that front; however, its president, Hastings Banda, would not permit it for fear both that his communication through Mozambique to the sea would be severed and that such activity would attract unwanted Portuguese, Rhodesian, and South African military incursions into his country. Eventually, however, Banda succumbed and gave tacit support in one of his tortuous changes in political direction.

Following Mondlane's assassination in June 1970 by dissidents in his party, FRELIMO, under its new, aggressive leader Samora Machel, began to move its troops to Zambia and develop a series of bases along the Zambian border north of the Zambesi River and in the Téte District of Mozambique. These forces transited Malawi with Banda turning a blind eye much to Portuguese distress.[5] Indeed, Al Venter notes that FRELIMO insurgents were traveling openly by the busload from Tanzania and were supported by the Malawi police, who were making certain that they did not linger there.[6] This development forced Portuguese attention to shift to the northeast.

Téte was, like Niassa and Cabo Delgado, a sparsely populated area. Within the district, however, Portugal had embarked on an ambitious project in 1969 at Cahora Bassa (variously Cabora Bassa) to dam the upper reaches of the Zambesi River as a source of inexpensive electrical power for Mozambique and South Africa.

Eduardo Mondlane. (Albert Grandolini Collection)

Samora Machel (Albert Grandolini Collection)

The dam was also designed to create an enormous reservoir 280 kilometres in length and 38 kilometres at its widest point.[7] This source would irrigate heretofore dry but fertile lands in an effort to bring prosperity to Téte and Mozambique and harness this income for the metrópole. This project and its lake were seen potentially as an effective block to FRELIMO infiltration through Téte and into Rhodesia and southern Mozambique. The dam construction site was also a tempting FRELIMO target. As it was, by 1971 FRELIMO was active in the area south of the Zambesi in Téte.[8] This FRELIMO presence resulted in attacks on Cahora Bassa and penetration southward.

Still by the end of the war in 1974, FRELIMO penetration of Mozambique was limited largely to Téte, Niassa, and Cabo Delgado, and was stalemated militarily. Over the years of fighting, FRELIMO had created support only among a small minority of the population in the north, and so few further south, that it was exceedingly difficult for it to govern Mozambique for decades afterward.

FRELIMO began with a disorganised force of uncertain strength and by the early 1970s had an active force of about 7,200 regulars and 2,400 popular militia.[9] As one would expect, Nyerere throughout the war controlled the flow of arms, munitions, and supplies from China, the Soviet Union, and Eastern Europe on behalf of FRELIMO, and this matériel was always plentiful.[10]

The first incident of armed action in Mozambique occurred on the evening of 21 August 1964, when an automobile took shots from a canhangulo, a home-made shotgun, while travelling on the Mueda–Mocímboa da Praia road. Fortunately, the occupants were only frightened and not hurt. Three days later, on 24 August, a group of FRELIMO operatives assassinated Father Daniel Boormans of the Dutch Catholic Mission at Bomela. The crime occurred next to the Mission of Nangololo, where there was a reunion of missionaries. Father Daniel was returning from the conference that evening accompanied by his verger Ernesto Dinagongo, when he was ambushed and shot with a canhangulo. His corpse was afterward beaten severely. A month later, on 24 September there was an assault by FRELIMO on the residence and secretariat of the small posto of Cobué in the Niassa district. This was followed on 26 September by a similar attack on the *posto* of Chai in the Cabo Delgado district, and this date is generally considered to be the beginning of hostilities in Mozambique.[11] The first FRELIMO attack on a military installation followed on 29 September with an assault on the base at Mueda characterised by two hours of light arms fire. The situation in Niassa and Cabo Delgado worsened day by day, and by early 1966 these two northern districts were in crisis.

THE HORSE CAVALRY SOLUTION

By September 1969 the war was a long way from ending. Populations of the northern districts of Téte, Niassa, and Cabo Delgado were subject to violent subversion, and this situation represented a difficult problem, despite a vigorous civil and military effort. Effectively projecting power, civil or military, was hampered by an inability to maintain and fill the necessary logistic lines of communication to and within these three northern districts and thus to support the needed offensives there.[12] General Kaúlza de Arriaga, the new ground force commander who had assumed his duties in July 1969, was looking for solutions to his power projection shortcomings and was open to new ideas. In this vein, Lieutenant Colonel Jorge Mathias, a cavalry officer who was serving a tour of duty in Mozambique at the time and who had participated in the creation of the horse cavalry units in Angola, undertook to produce a twenty-one page study detailing his thoughts on the potential of establishing such units in Mozambique.[13]

Mathias generally followed the rationale behind the argument for cavalry in Angola and saw its use in securing a region and in acting as an intervention force. Area security, it was argued, would be achieved by reconnaissance, and presence through patrolling. Intervention would be achieved through the mobility of the horse in sweeping the area in coordination with other complementary forces and through its ability to intimidate and shock foot soldiers. Mathias cited the comparatively low cost of cavalry and offered figures on horse purchases from Argentina. The horse was at a disadvantage, he noted, in dense undergrowth, steep and rocky terrain, and marshland, as had been researched and experienced in Angola.[14] This last observation placed the useful orbit of cavalry in the highland regions of Mozambique inland from the Indian Ocean coast.

The proposal by Mathias gained traction, and in August 1972 a request was made to the Ministers of the Army and of National Defence to authorise the creation of a cavalry squadron in the Military Region of Mozambique (Região Militar de Moçambique or

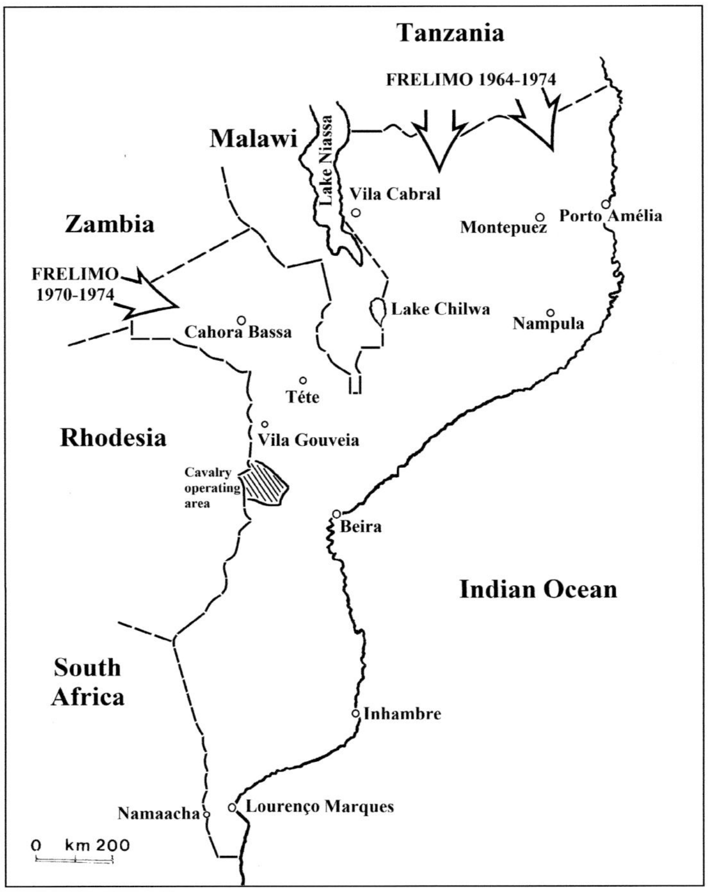

FRELIMO Lines of Penetration and Cavalry Operating Area. (Map by the author)

RMM). The squadron would be located at the Centre of Instruction at Vila Pery (Centro de Instrução de Vila Pery or CIVP), and the stand-up phase would be overseen by Major Alberto Mourão da Costa Ferreira, who would head a Reception Committee consisting of Alferes Sardinha, Alferes Martins Alves, and Alferes (Veterinarian) Carriço da Conceição.[15] The selection of Vila Pery paralleled that of Silva Porto in that both were in the interior highland plains of the country where the climate was pleasant and cool, and the terrain only slightly rugged with large open areas of grass broken by chana-like plains, rivers and annaras.[16] Both were served by railway lines, in the case of Silva Porto, the CFB, and in the case of Vila Pery, the Caminho de Ferro de Beira, and a highway that paralleled each railway. The greater advantage of Vila Pery was its proximity to Umtali, the third largest city in Rhodesia, which was only ninety kilometres distant and contained shops with everything one could possibly want to outfit a horse and rider.[17] Silva Porto was more isolated in the middle of Angola and for this reason was called "Silva Morto" (Silva Dead).

It is difficult to know exactly at what level the decision was made on the request, that of the commander-in-chief or of a local headquarters, but within only fifteen days the proposal was approved and the first thirty-six remounts arrived from Rhodesia supplied by the firm Equizad in Bulawaio. The sudden arrival of the horses caught the newly established Reception Committee completely unprepared.[18] In all some 164 horses were purchased in Rhodesia and arrived at Vila Pery between August 1972 and March 1973 on six different occasions.[19] Because the decision to purchase and ship the horses to Vila Pery was made without coordination, the Committee had to scramble to accommodate the new arrivals. The poor quality of available feed and the lack of equipment and infrastructure compounded the difficulties. Hastily arranged sheds were holed in the roof and sides by rust so much so that when it rained, the water fell on top of the horses and on their mangers. This led to contamination of the already poor feed and hazarded the health of the horses through indigestion. The floor became soaked in rainwater, manure, and urine with the effect of burying the horses' feet in contaminated mud up to the fetlock joint and causing a rotting of the hooves. Under these conditions the horses showed health instability and a nervousness manifested in their failing to lie down to rest and acquiring the bad habit of gnawing at the mangers and stalls. This behaviour caused weight-loss and hampered their recuperation. Consequently, there was an urgency to build the proper housing for the animals.[20] As to equipment, halters were in short supply, and those available were quite worn. This made management of the horses difficult.

Construction of squadron stables and attendant buildings was verbally authorised in the fall of 1972 after the first shipment of horses. These included a stable for sixty horses, office for the commanding officer, a secretariat, a veterinary section, a post office, and an arsenal.[21] Other services, such as an infirmary, a petrol station, and a communications centre, would be furnished by CIVP. There was no chaplain. Another primary shortcoming was the laundry facility that was supposed to serve some 900 men at the height of instruction in Vila Pery.[22] The establishment of this infrastructure took time, and its initial absence was highly disruptive.

In the rush to stand up the squadron, Costa Ferreira modelled it after the experiences gained in Angola without adequate reflection. Blindly accepting these without considering the specific local conditions often led to problems. For instance, leaving the horses unshod did not work, and the Mozambican terrain quickly disabused everyone of this practice. Just as the adaptation of horse cavalry to counterinsurgency in eastern Angola was specific to that battlefield, so it would have to be specific to the highlands of Mozambique. This awkward beginning contrasted sharply with that in Silva Porto with the experimental platoon.[23]

The greatest problems came from the rush to assemble and train the force. The abrupt delivery of the initial remounts to an unprepared site was only the beginning. Four weeks into instruction, the program was plagued by a deficiency in riding tack, a lack of qualified instructors, and the low quality of the recruits. In Angola it required three months to train a trooper and to make him combat ready. The initial six weeks of this period consisted of basic military training and riding lessons. In Mozambique, however, this was complicated by the low educational and behavioural levels of the available recruits, as recruiting and training had not been well considered. In contrast to the Angolan recruits who were chosen from the Cuamatos and Cuanhamas, tribes that had traditionally raised cattle and were familiar with large animals, the men for the initial platoon in Mozambique were chosen from basic recruits who had failed the final phase of their military training.[24] On one occasion only 38 soldiers of 142 available met the minimum requirements for joining a cavalry unit.[25] The result was that additional instruction and education were necessary in such basics as daily hygiene, first aid, comportment, and the Portuguese language, and these significantly extended the initial training period.

The second phase was to be dedicated to learning the capabilities of the horse and building a relationship with him such that horse and rider became a team, and it was projected to last six weeks. Sadly, the basics of the first phase were not fully mastered by a majority of recruits, so this horse-rider teamwork phase progressed irregularly. It was perhaps unrealistic to expect such men who could not look

Stables under construction at Vila Pery. (Colonel Castro Neves Collection)

Stables take shape at Vila Pery. (Colonel Castro Neves Collection)

Interior of completed stables at Vila Pery. (Colonel Castro Neves Collection)

after themselves to care and manage a large and noble animal with the capacity to serve uncomplainingly to death. One of the great obstacles, it was discovered, was a lack of general affection and appreciation of the horse in the recruits, a necessary characteristic of a cavalryman. For instance, the recruits tended to be brusque with their mounts, and it was difficult to teach them otherwise, as they held no innate sympathetic feeling for the animals.[26] More than 90 percent of the soldiers were very hard on their horses' mouths to the point of unacceptably violent behaviour and used the reins with little feel or sensitivity.[27] The subtle notion of steering the mount with a light rein and leg pressure was generally lost on the recruits, and this lack of understanding resulted in numerous accidents.[28] This void in empathy meant that recruits took an unusually long time to learn management of the horse. Hence training such recruits to a useful level required an extraordinary amount of time and patience to overcome both the lack of aptitude and the periodic student relapses, and only in the long term would positive results be evident. The goal was to produce not only horsemen but soldiers able to fight dismounted, a seemingly ambitious one in light of the slow, laboured, and irregular progress.[29]

The recruits struggled to master formation marches in lines and columns, again because of the slow mastery of communication with the horse. Maintaining control of the horse and building his confidence in his rider was slow to materialise and made managing him under strange or stressful circumstances a challenge. Helicopters, gunfire, and the other sounds of war would unsettle a horse, unless he were properly acclimated and had confidence in his rider. As to training the Rhodesian horses for combat, training the remounts occurred alongside that of the recruits. Most of the animals were comfortable with bursts of automatic fire as close as twenty metres. Some, however, shied at the sight of a G-3 or the noise of a handwheel. Again, like the recruits, these remounts required protracted training.[30]

The few qualified instructors worked long hours, yet the low quality of available recruits posed continuing problems for all involved: horses, instructors, and trainees.[31] The solution was seen as importing more experienced personnel from the metrópole to be integrated into the proposed unit to provide a reservoir of experience and a sense of the "cavalry spirit" so lacking.[32] The instructors saw no other way of advancing beyond basic equitation to field formations and tactics. The assignment of Major Castro Neves, who would eventually command the squadron, proved the solution to many of these problems, as his leadership and competence potentially provided the needed bridge to success. Still, success was elusive.

The third and final phase, which featured an 80 to 100-kilometre battle course test to improve the trooper's skills in the field was a still a work-in-progress, even as the squadron was supposedly battle-ready. Nevertheless, the prospective unit was inordinately slow to learn and even after the 1st Cavalry Squadron (1° Esquadrão a Cavalo) was formally established in February 1973, five months after its authorisation, with 183 men, 172 horses, and eight vehicles, its recruits were still not trained to the standard of those in Angola over a similar period.[33] The lack of qualified instructors in combination with the low quality of recruits continued to stall progress. Training continued to advance slowly and agonisingly. By September 1973, however, a series of operations was initiated in an attempt to complete the third phase over the next five months. These were conducted in an area where there was little chance of encountering any enemy, and if encountered, he would be lightly armed and number few, something that the unit might be capable of handling. The troopers would primarily police the assigned exercise area, which centred on the Púngue River some 25 kilometres to the north of Vila Pery, and practice making contact with the population.[34] In all there were sixteen such missions with an average duration of five days each. In one case a patrol did encounter a group of three enemy armed with canhangulos and in another destroyed ten presumed enemy huts.[35] During these training operations the patrols worked primarily in two sections, totalling between 36 and 40 mounted troopers. On occasion training patrols were expanded and conducted by a three-platoon group. A platoon, again as in Angola, consisted of three sections of thirteen mounted troopers each plus a support section of one machine gunner, three rifle grenadiers, an orderly, a bugler, and a farrier. The sections in Mozambique were slightly larger at 18 to 20 troopers each. Its deployment followed traditional cavalry formations and tactics with adaptations to the Mozambican battlefield. By March 1974, only 109 horses out of a total available of 132 were ready for operations.[36]

General Kaúlza de Arriaga, Commander-in-Chief of the Armed Forces in Mozambique, visits the headquarters of the newly established 1st Cavalry Squadron at Vila Pery. (Colonel Castro Neves Collection)

CAVALRY OPERATIONS

With this troubled beginning, the squadron from February 1974 began to execute its mission:

- Conduct offensive and defensive military operations, combatting armed bands of guerrillas and pseudo-regular enemy (FRELIMO) forces,
- Conduct psychological operations (PSYOP) against the enemy and in support of the population, and
- Support the civil authorities when requested in accordance with directives.[37]

As operations unfolded over the next eight weeks before the Carnation Revolution of 25 April, a successful coup against the Caetano government by a group of mid-level officers, the squadron conducted twenty-two patrols. In none of these was there any contact with the enemy. It found no enemy bases, and thus did not assault any. Nor were any other forces able to detect an enemy presence within the squadron operating area, despite references to the presence of armed groups there. If any were present, then they were highly mobile and dispersed and had no fixed bases. Still, the intense patrolling activity of the squadron and its mere presence created a climate of uncertainty and insecurity for the enemy and prevented him from establishing any foothold.[38] This cavalry presence gave the population confidence in its security and the ability of the Portuguese forces to protect it from enemy depredation. The squadron regularly patrolled the road network and known travel routes as well as the Beira railroad and its adjacent terrain. To this was added the large agricultural properties and other key terrain.[39]

General Kaúlza de Arriaga, Commander-in-Chief of the Armed Forces in Mozambique on an inspection tour of the stables in July 1973. (Colonel Castro Neves Collection)

General Kaúlza de Arriaga, Commander-in-Chief of the Armed Forces in Mozambique, awards the distinctive cavalry cap or *bivaque* in a ceremony at squadron headquarters at Vila Pery. (Colonel Castro Neves Collection)

General Kaúlza de Arriaga, Commander-in-Chief of the Armed Forces in Mozambique, in conversation with a recruit who undergoing training. (Colonel Castro Neves Collection)

From time to time the patrols faced difficult terrain in the general operating area that was bounded to the north by the Púngue River and to the south by the Revué River. To the west was the

Rhodesian border, and to the east the lowlands beyond Inchope. This area had few north-south water courses for orientation, and those that had to be crossed had soft and muddy banks. The land can be mountainous, making visual reconnaissance difficult. In places the terrain is rugged and dangerous with dense vegetation that is difficult to circumnavigate. In others, it is rolling farmland with great cultivated extensions bounded by barbed wire or other fencing.[40] In the dry season (May to October) finding water for horses was always difficult, and as a consequence, patrols were conducted between known water sources, and these were largely towns or villages.[41] In the rainy season (November to April) thunder and torrential downpours made the horses nervous and robbed them of their needed rest and made them tired.[42] Many times the force would be loaded into rail cars and transported to the initial point of their patrol. This was done, as in Angola, to save the horses and men from spending themselves in transit to the operating area for the patrol.

While the squadron patrolled this area regularly, it never held any direct or even indirect contact with the enemy.[43] Yet, the "cavalry spirit" was missing. As Captain Rosério da Silva Guilherme, the last commander of the squadron, lamented, "Not in all cases, but perhaps in a few, the conditions of the terrain might be considered in justifying the small (or negligible) operational yield and the exaggerated fatigue of the horses."[44] As to the fatigue of the horses, none of the patrols were lengthy in the sense of those conducted in Angola, so the supposed fatigue was more of a perception on the part of the troopers than an understanding that these were war horses that needed to be pushed to the limits of their capabilities.

The squadron conducted 33 additional operations through the Carnation Revolution, and thereafter a further 110.[45] These short daily operations concluded on 30 September of that year, when the squadron was decommissioned. Reports of these operations reflect a new unit struggling to overcome inexperience and severe deficiencies in training and personnel. Sadly, after the revolution political and military developments made it impossible to confirm the usefulness of horse cavalry units in Mozambique. It had been a well-intentioned effort that came to naught.

The 1st Cavalry Squadron on parade at its headquarters at Vila Pery. (Colonel Castro Neves Collection)

Standing instructor with seated student demonstrating the clearing of a small jump at the 1st Cavalry Squadron. (Colonel Castro Neves Collection)

5
HORSE CAVALRY IN COUNTERINSURGENCY

Horse cavalry forces from the beginning of their operations in 1966, and particularly after augmentation in 1968, helped to neutralize MPLA operations in central and eastern Angola and presented a continuing threat to insurgent activity. Their large, sweeping patrols found the enemy in the vast plains of Angola and destroyed him. It was not spectacular work, but it was decisive in guaranteeing the security of the population and enabling the people to lead normal lives. Cavalry was particularly effective in its psychological impact on the enemy. The mobility and quickness of reaction, especially to an ambush, was intimidating. A cavalry formation charging at a gallop and surrounding an insurgent force or pursuing it was decisive and generally successful in its action. Horses moved silently through the savanna plains relative to the helicopter and were able to surprise the insurgents quite well, and thus had better success in detecting guerrillas in the bush than helicopter-borne troops. They were not only capable of moving over vast distances during a patrol, and 500 kilometres was not considered unusual, but also of negotiating the most inaccessible and remote territory. In moving against an enemy force, they exhibited flexibility with the combination of an approach by horse and the transition to attack or reconnaissance on foot.[1]

These Portuguese cavalry operations represented a partial solution to the problem of covering approximately 250,000 square kilometres of miserable terrain, normally impassable in the rainy season. With some 300 cavalry troops and a minimum of logistic strain the Portuguese were able to gather intelligence, communicate with the population, provide a presence, and conduct operations between the larger, full-scale offenses against MPLA infiltration in the east. Only in Rhodesia with the establishment of Grey's Scouts in 1976 did a modern counterinsurgency employ horse cavalry as a solution to its mobility requirements in the way that the Portuguese did.[2]

Beginning in 1977, the South African Defence Force (SADF) used cavalry and scrambler motorcycles for hot pursuit of guerrillas in its border war with SWAPO (South-West African People's Organisation), which was concluded in 1989. This SADF use was quite different from the long-range patrolling of the Portuguese in

Troopers in the field near Vila Pery practicing patrolling techniques. (Colonel Castro Neves Collection)

Recruits learning to wash their mounts in a tributary to the River Revué near Vila Pery. (Colonel Castro Neves Collection)

Recruits of the 1st Cavalry Squadron practicing horsemanship at its headquarters at Vila Pery. (Colonel Castro Neves Collection)

Angola. All three of these cavalry employments were successful in their own way; however, there were limitations. Under heavy fire a horse could panic and throw his rider. While there were few equine deserters, nevertheless, this risk was present. The use of horses was also restricted to tsetse-free areas, a significantly limiting condition. Horses, like humans, could become sick. This incapacity was no less serious than a mechanical failure on a vehicle, and the training, care, and feeding of the animals was no more arduous or expensive than maintaining the same vehicle. In fact, the use of motorcycles by the SADF revealed that the horse, while not as fast, was more durable. Motorcycles in the bush tended to have a short life.[3] While such mechanical devices were useful, the mounted trooper could range much farther afield over difficult terrain than most vehicles, and certainly farther than his comrade on foot, without becoming exhausted, even in hot weather. His perspective from atop a steed gave him a distinct advantage over the guerrilla. The horse moved silently through the bush and gave mounted security forces the advantage of surprise. Finally, the most compelling argument for resurrecting the archaic horse soldier lay in the unique advantage of combining troop mobility with the maintenance of contact with the population.

Portugal's resources were stretched thin in fighting the Campaigns. In the 1970 period the nineteen Alouette helicopters and the two newly acquired SA.330 Pumas represented thin resources to cover the estimated 400,000 square kilometres of Angola's eastern front.[4] The addition of the dragoons produced a winning, cost-effective, low-key combination with the helicopters and infantrymen that helped to result in a neutralization of the enemy in the east.

SELECTED BIBLIOGRAPHY

História da Unidade – 1° Esquadrão a Cavalo/RMM [Unit History – 1st Squadron of Cavalry/RMM], (Lissabon: Estado Maior do Exército, 1981)

Afonso, Aniceto, and Carlos de Matos Gomes. *Guerra Colonial* [Colonial War], (Lissabon: Notícias, 2001)

Abbott, Peter, and Manuel Ribeiro Rodrigues. *Modern African Wars (2): Angola and Mozambique 1961–74*, (Oxford: Osprey, 1988)

Binda, Alexandre. *The Equus Men, Rhodesia's Mounted Infantry: The Grey's Scouts 1896–1980* (Solihull: Helion and Co., 2015)

Cordeiro, Arsénio Raposo, *Lusitano Horse: Son of the Wind*, (Lissabon: Edições Inapa, 2002)

Dias de Almeida, Carlos Manuel, "O Esquadrão a Cavalao de Moçambique ne Guerra do Ultramar." [The Cavalry Squadron of Mozambique in the War of the Ultramar]. *Revista da Cavalaria* (March 2009), pp. 20–27.

Ferrand d'Almeida, António Casimiro, "Recorddações de um 'Dragão de Angola'" [Recollections of a "Dragoon of Angola"], *Revista Militar* (October–November 1985), pp. 689–719.

Mateus, Henrique, "A Acção da Cavalaria no Leste de Angola." [Cavalry Operations in the East of Angola], *Revista da Cavalaria* (March 2009), pp. 12–19.

Ollivier, Patrick, *Commandos de Brousse* [Bush Commandos], (Paris: Bernard Grasset, 1985).

Steenkamp, Willem. *South Africa's Border War 1966-1989*, (Gibraltar: Ashanti Publishing Limited, 1989)

van der Waals, Willem S., *Portugal's War in Angola 1961–1974*, (Rivonia: Ashanti Publishing, 1993)

NOTES

Chapter 1

1 António Casimiro Ferrand d'Almeida, "Recorddações de um 'Dragão de Angola'" [Recollections of a "Dragoon of Angola"], *Revista Militar* (October–November 1985): pp. 690–692.

2 Alberto da Costa e Silva, *A Manilha e o Libambo: A África e a Escravidão, de 1500 a 1700* [The Manilha and the Limbambo: Africa and Slavery, from 1500 to 1700] (Rio de Janeiro: Nova Fronteira, 2011).

3 Arsénio Raposo Cordeiro, *Lusitano Horse: Son of the Wind* (Lisbon: Edições Inapa, 2002), p. 1.

4 Ibid., p. 8

5 Ibid.

6 Ibid.

7 Charles W.C. Oman, *A History of the Art of War in the Sixteenth Century* (London: Greenhill, 1999), p. 51.

8 David Nicolle, *The Portuguese in the Age of Discovery c.1340–1665* (Botley, United Kingdom: Osprey, 2012), p. 35.

9 Ibid, p. 23.

10 Ibid.

11 Charles R. Boxer, *The Portuguese Seaborne Empire, 1415–1825* (New York: Alfred A. Knopf, 1969), p. 19.

12 Ibid., p. 25.

13 Ibid.

14 William C. Atkinson, "Introduction" to Luís Vaz de Camões, *The Lusiads*, trans. William C. Atkinson (Harmondsworth: Penguin Books, 1952), pp. 19-20.

15 Ibid., p. 20.

16 W. Gervase Clarence-Smith, *The Third Portuguese Empire 1825–1975: A Study in Economic Imperialism* (Manchester: Manchester University Press, 1985), p. 1. The author argues that while politicians and colonial ideologues were able to play strongly on this vibrant chord of imperial grandeur throughout the history of the Third Portuguese Empire (1825–1975) by recalling the great days of the discoveries and Asian conquests, the Portuguese citizens themselves were never unanimous in their attitudes toward Portuguese Asia, and many saw it as a hollow triumph that drained the country of resources and left it impotent in its defence against Spain.

17 Ibid., p. 2. The author argues that Brazil was a far different enterprise than the earlier Asian experience in that it had provided raw materials and in turn Portugal had supplied manufactures. It also had been a colony of settlement rather than one where "immigrants died of tropical diseases and melted into the local population."

18 Toby Michael Ormsby Redgrave, "Wellington's Logistical Arrangements in the Peninsula War 1809–14" (PhD thesis, King's College London, 1979), p. 91.

19 David Birmingham, *A Concise History of Portugal* (Cambridge: Cambridge University Press, 1993), p. 140.

20 Malyn Newitt, *A History of Mozambique* (London: Hurst & Co., 1995), p. 347

21 Eric Axelson, *Portugal and the Scramble for Africa 1875-1891* (Johannesburg: Witwatersrand University Press, 1967), pp. 211-213.

22 David M. Abshire and Michael A. Samuels, *Portuguese Africa: A Handbook* (New York: Praeger Publishers, 1969), p. 72.

23 Newitt, *A History of Mozambique,* p. 348.

24 Abshire and Samuels, *Portuguese Africa,* p. 74.

25 Ibid.

26 António José Telo, *Os Açores e o Controlo do Atlântico (1898–1948)* [The Azores and Control of the Atlantic (1898–1948) (Porto: Edições ASA, 1993), pp. 87–88.

27 Helmuth Stoecker, ed., *German Imperialism in Africa*, trans. Bernd Zöllner (London: C. Hurst & Co., 1986), pp. 251–252.

28 David Martelo, *As Mágoas do Império* [The Sorrows of Empire] (Mem Martins, Portugal: Publicações Europa-America, 1998), p. 228.

29 Carlos Leitão Carreira, "Escola Prática de Cavalaria" [Practical School of Cavalry], *Recuemos* (21 September 2006): p. 2.

30 Antoine Fortuné de Brack, *Cavalry Outpost Duties*, trans. Camillo Casatti Cadmus Carr (New York: John Wiley & Sons, 1893), pp. 46–50.

31 Ibid.

32 Douglas L. Wheeler, "Joaquim Mouzinho de Albuquerque (1855–1902) e a Política do Colonialismo" [Joaquim Mouzinho de Albuquerque (1855–1902) and Colonial Policy], *Análise Social* XVI (1980): p. 296.

33 Ibid., p. 297.

34 Ibid.

35 René Pélissier, *Naissance du Mozambique, Tome 1: Résistance et Révoltes Anticoloniales (1854–1918)* (Orgeval: Pélissier, 1984), p. 13.

36 Ibid., p. 299.

37 René Pélissier, *Naissance du Mozambique, Tome 2: Résistance et Révoltes Anticoloniales (1854–1918)*, (Orgeval: Pélissier, 1984), p. 630.

38 Douglas L. Wheeler, "Joaquim Mouzinho de Albuquerque," p. 301.

39 Ibid.

40 René Pélissier, *Naissance du Mozambique, Tome 2*, p. 615.

41 Ibid.

42 Ibid.

43 Ibid., p. 631.

44 José Bento Rosa da Silva, "Revolta da Vacina 'Made in Africa': Moçâmedes–1897" [Revolt of the Vaccine "Made in Africa": Moçâmedes–1897], *Revista de História da África e de Estudos da Diáspora Africana* 8 (December 2011): pp. 127–128.

45 René Pélissier, *Les Guerres Grises* (Orgeval: Pélissier, 1977), p. 438

46 Fernando Augusto da Silva Guardado, "O Massacre dos Dragões do Conde de Almoster" [The Massacre of the Dragoons of Conde de Almoster], in *Cadernos Coloniais No. 34* (Lisbon: Cosmos, 1939), p. 4.

47 Ibid., p. 8–9. Not only was horse sickness a deadly problem but the prevalence of the tsetse fly, the vector of trypanosomiasis, made the health of horses in the lowlands of Angola and other tropical areas haphazard. See also Humphrey J. Fisher, "'He Swalloweth the Ground with Fierceness and Rage': The Horse in the Central Sudan I, Its Introduction" *Journal of African History*, XIII, 3 (1972): pp. 369–388; Humphrey J. Fisher, "'He Swalloweth the Ground with Fierceness and Rage': The Horse in the Central Sudan II, Its Use" *Journal of African History*, XIV, 3 (1973): pp. 355–379; and Robin Law, "A West African Cavalry State: The Kingdom of Oyo," *Journal of African History*, XVI, 1 (1975): pp. 1–15.

48 Pélissier, *Les Guerres Grises,* p. 438.

49 Ibid., p. 439.

50 Ibid., p. 451.

51 Ibid., p. 452.

52 Jaime Ferreira Regalado, *Cuamatos, 1907: Os Bravos de Mufilo no Sul de Angola* [Cuamatos, 1907: The Valient of Mufilo in the South of Angola] (Lisbon: Tribuna da História, 2004), front flyleaf.

53 Ibid., p. 25.

54 Ibid., p. 49.

55 Pélissier, *Les Guerres Grises,* p. 465.

56 Alberto de Almeida Teixeira, *Roçadas na Ocupação do Sul de Angola, Pelo Império No. 4* [Roçadas in the Occupation of the South of Angola, About the Empire No. 4] (Lisbon: Agência Geral das Colónias, 1935), pp. 46–47.

57 Regalado, *Cuamatos, 1907,* p. 53.

58 Pélissier, *Les Guerres Grises,* p. 466.

59 Ibid.

60 Regalado, *Cuamatos, 1907,* p. 89.

61 Augusto Casimiro, *Naulila* (Lisbon: Seara Nova, 1922), p. 65

62 Bello de Almeida, *Meio Seculo de Lutas no Ultramar: Subsidios para a História das Campanhas do Exército Portuguez de Terra e Mar no Império Colonial* [Half a Century of Struggles in the *Ultramar*: Aid to the History of Portuguese Army Campaigns on Land and Sea in the Colonial Empire] (Lisbon: Sociedade de Geografia de Lisboa, 1937), pp. 88–90. The two squadrons were the 3rd Squadron/RC9 and 1st Squadron of the Dragoons of Angola.

63 Manuel de Oliveira Gomes da Costa, *A Guerra nas Colonias* (Lisbon: Arthur Brandão, 1922), pp. 51–52.

64 António Fernandes Varão, *Investidas Alemãs de Angola* [German Incursions of Angola] (Lisbon: Lucas & Co., 1934), pp. 12–14.

65 Miguel Freire, "Naulila – Quando o inimigo ainda não o era, mas já se combatia" [Naulila – When the enemy no longer existed but still fought], in *A Grande Guerra: Um Século Depois* [The Great War: A Century Afterward], ed. António José Telo (Lisbon: Academia Militar, 2014), p. 131.

66 Casimiro, *Naulila,* pp. 97–98.

67 Ibid.

68 Belo de Almeida, *Meio Seculo de Lutas no Ultramar,* p. 90.

69 Casimiro, *Naulila,* p. 95.

70 Ibid., p. 98.

71 Ibid., pp. 99–101.

72 Filipe Ribeiro de Meneses, *Portugal 1914–1926: From the First World War to Military Dictatorship* (Bristol: H/PLAM, 2004), p. 36.

73 Ibid.

74 There were 69 Portuguese dead: 3 officers and 66 soldiers, of which 54 were European; 76 wounded: 5 officers and 71 soldiers, of which 61 were European; 37 prisoners: 3 officers and 34 European soldiers. For their part, the Germans had 12 Europeans killed, of which 2 were officers, and 30

wounded, of which 10 were officers.
75 Ribeiro de Meneses, *Portugal 1914–1926,* p. 36.
76 Réne Pélissier, "Campagnes Militaires au Sud-Angola (1885–1915)," *Cahiers d'Etudes Africaines* 9 (1969), p. 52.
77 António Pereira de Eça, *Campanha do Sul de Angola em 1915, Report* [Campaign for the South of Angola in 1915, Report] (Lisbon: Imprensa Nacional, 1923), pp. 490–491, and 494.
78 Pélissier, "Campagnes Militaires au Sud-Angola (1885–1915)," p. 55.
79 Ibid., p. 53.
80 Ibid., p. 57.
81 Ibid.
82 Ibid., p. 54.
83 Ibid.
84 Ibid., p. 56.
85 Ibid.
86 Ibid.
87 René Pélissier, *Naissance du Mozambique, Tome 2,* p. 676.
88 Ibid., p. 688.
89 António Paulo David Silva Duarte, "Esboço para uma Leitura Estratégica sobre a Campanha de Moçambique (1914-1918)," *Revista Militar* (August/September 1998): p. 673.
90 Mário Costa, *É o inimigo qui fala: Subsídios inéditos para oestudo da Campanha da África Oriental, 1914-1918* (Lourenço Marques: Imprensa Nacional, 1932), pp. 19–20.
91 Silva Duarte, "Esboço para uma Leitura Estratégica sobre a Campanha de Moçambique", pp. 677–678.
92 Ibid.
93 Ibid.
94 Alberto M. Simões, *Condenados, A Grande Guerra Vivida às Portas do Delgado* [Doomed, The Great War Lived at the Doors of the Sleazy] (Aveiro: Tipografia Lusitânia, 1933), p. 27. Translation of the quotation is by Anna Paula Soares Pires.
95 Manuel de Oliveira Gomes da Costa, *A Guerra nas Colonias* (Lisbon: Arthur Brandão, 1922), p. 67. Francisco Barreto led expeditions up the Zambesi River in 1570 and 1573 that were severely reduced by sickness and a hostile population.
96 Carlos Selvagem, *Tropa d'África* (Pôrto: Renascença Portuguesa, 1919), p. 97.
97 Ibid.
98 Gomes da Costa, *A Guerra nas Colonias*, p. 68.
99 Carlos Gomes Bessa, *O Combate de Muíte: Aspectos Relacionados com a Participação Portuguesa na Guerra de 1914–18 em Moçambique* [The Combat at Muíte: Aspects Related to the Portuguese Participation in the War of of 1914–18 in Mozambique] (Lisbon: Academia Portuguesa da História, 1984), p. 148.
100 Gomes da Costa, *A Guerra nas Colonias*, p. 226.
101 E.A. Azambuja Martins, *Nevala, Expedição a Moçambique* [Nevala, Expedition to Mozambique] (Lisbon: Famalicão, 1935), p. 254.
102 Ibid.
103 Gomes da Costa, *A Guerra nas Colonias*, p. 255.
104 Albert Henry Trapmann, "The Cycle in Warfare: Its Potency as a Strategical and Tactical Factor," Paper read at the Royal United Service Institute, London, 16 December 1908.
105 Ribeiro de Meneses, *Portugal 1914–1926*, pp. 66–67.
106 Miguel Freire, "Dragoons of Angola," *Osprey Military Journal* 4, issue 4: p. 50.
107 Ibid., p. 45.
108 Lieutenant Colonel of Cavalry Vincente da Silva, "Lances de «Cavalo» no «Xadrez» Angolano" [Moves of the «Knight» on the Angolan «Chessboard»], *Journal do Exército* (June 1972): p. 28.
109 Colonel of Cavalry César Augusto Rodrigues Mano, interview by the author, 10 November 1994, Oeiras, Portugal. Colonel Mano commanded the *Grupo de Dragões de Angola* between 1973 and 1974.
110 Ibid.
111 Ibid.

Chapter 2

1 Marcello Caetano, "Editorial," *O Mundo Português* [Portuguese World], 2 (1935): p. 218.
2 John A. Marcum, *The Angolan Revolution, Vol. I: The Anatomy of an Explosion (1950–1962)* (Cambridge, Mass.: MIT Press, 1969), pp. 347–351. Marcum lists some fifty-nine groups affecting Angola alone beginning in the 1940s and either merging with one another or vanishing by 1962.
3 Malyn Newitt, *Portugal in Africa: The Last Hundred Years* (London: C. Hurst & Co., 1981), p. 190.
4 Douglas L. Wheeler and René Pélissier, *Angola* (London: Pall Mall Press, 1971), p. 167. The authors cite as an example the Congo district in 1960. For its 37,000 square miles it had fourteen *concelhos* (basic urban or semi-urban administrative unit) or *circunscrições* (basic rural administrative division) and thirty-seven posts, for an average of 725 square miles per administrative division. This presence would hardly be effective in controlling a frontier, as the posts would be dozens of miles apart. Large numbers of people could and did cross undetected.
5 António Lopes Pires Nunes, *Angola 1961: Da Baixa do Cassange a Nambuangongo* [Angola 1961: From Baixa do Cassange to Nambuangongo] (Lisbon: Prefácio, 2005), pp. 86–87.
6 Ibid.
7 Ibid.
8 Ibid.
9 René Pélissier, *Le Naufrage des Caravelles: Etudes sur la Fin de l'Empire Portuguais (1961–1975)* [The Shipwreck of the Caravels: Studies on the End of the Portuguese Empire] (Orgeval: Editions Pélissier, 1979, p. 147; Tomás George Conceição Silva, "The Portuguese Air Force in the African Wars of 1961–1974" in *Memories of Portugal's African Wars, 1961–1974* edited by John P. Cann (Quantico: Marine Corps University Foundation, 1998), p. 113; and Alexandra Correia, "O Dia da Barbárie" [The Day of Barbary], *Visão História* 12 (June 2011): p. 59.
10 Willem S. van der Waals, *Portugal's War in Angola 1961–1974* (Rivonia: Ashanti Publishing, 1993), p. 64.
11 Pélissier, *Naufrage des Caravelles,* p. 147.
12 Edgar Pereira da Costa Cardoso, *Presença da Força Aérea em Angola* [Presence of the Air Force in Angola] (Lisbon: Secretaria de Estado de Aeronáutica, 1963), p. 90.
13 Ibid., p. 91.
14 René Pélissier, *La Colonie du Minotaure: Nationalismes et Révoltes en Angola (1926–1961)* [The Colony of the Minotaur: Nationalist Movements and Revolts in Angola (1926–1961)] (Orgeval: Editions Pélissier, 1978, pp. 657–660; and van der Waals, *Portugal's War in Angola*, pp. 58–61.
15 Manuel Diogo Neto, "Acontecimentos no Norte de Angola" [Events in the North of Angola] *Mais Alto* 30 (June–July 1961): p. 9.
16 Ibid., p. 8.
17 René Pélissier, *La Colonie du Minotaure,* p. 658.
18 Ibid., pp. 657–660; van der Waals, *Portugal's War in Angola,* pp. 58–61.
19 Willem S. van der Waals, *Portugal's War in Angola*, p. 97. The author argues that Portuguese propaganda and social work among the refugees in Angola persuaded most of these displaced people to move into controlled settlements. This development deprived ELNA of popular support. ELNA had concentrated on military action in a human desert and on preventing MPLA infiltration. It had neglected to indoctrinate, organise, and win recruits among refugees returning to Angola and thus missed an opportunity to undermine Portuguese authority. Consequently no ELNA internal political infrastructure was established in Angola. Portugal gained the upper hand and maintained superior momentum until 1974.
20 Ibid.
21 Shola Adenekan, "Holden Roberto," *The New Black Magazine,* 22 October 2007, http://www.thenewblackmagazine.com/view.aspx?index=1042 (accessed 29 November 2018).
22 Ibid.
23 *Expresso* (Lisbon), 17 September 1974, p. 18.
24 Piero Gleijeses, *Conflicting Missions: Havana, Washington, and Africa 1959–1976* (Chapel Hill: University of North Carolina Press, 2002), p. 238.
25 Ibid.
26 John A. Marcum, *The Angolan Revolution, Volume II: Exile Politics and Insurgent Warfare (1962–1976)* (Cambridge: MIT Press, 1978), 42.
27 António Pires Nunes, *Angola 1966–74, Vitória Militar no Leste* [Angola 1966–74, Military Victory in the East] (Lisbon: Prefácio, 2002), p. 10.
28 Ibid.
29 Ricardo Cubas, "Um Destacamento Atribulado" [A Painful Detachment], *Mais Alto* 323 (January–February 2000): p. 36.
30 António Pires Nunes, *Siroco, Os Comandos no Leste de Angola* (Lisbon: Associação de Comandos, 2013), p. 45.
31 Comissão para o Estudo das Campanhas de África (1961–1974), *Resenha Histórico-Militar das Campanhas de África (1961–1974), 2° Volume, Dispositivo das Nossas Forças, Angola* [Historical-Military Report of the African Campaigns (1961–1974), 2° Volume, Disposition of Our Forces, Angola] (Lisbon, Estado-Maior do Exército, 1989), p. 127.
32 Pires Nunes, *Angola 1966–74,* p. 26.
33 Ibid., p. 40.
34 Ibid.
35 Comissão para o Estudo das Campanhas de África, *Resenha Histórico-Militar das Campanhas de África 1961–1974, 6 Volume, Tomo I, Angola–Livro 2,* p. 353.
36 Ibid.
37 Ibid.
38 Adelino Gomes, "Exército e UNITA Colaboraram antes de 74" [Army and UNITA Collaborate before 74], *Público* (19 December 1995), 2-4; and Óscar Cardoso, "Criador dos Flechas" [Creator of the Flechas] in José Freire Antunes, *A Guerra de África, 1961–1974, Volume 1* [The War in Africa, 1961–1974, Volume 1] (Lisbon: Temas e Debates, 1996), pp. 409–410.
39 Dalila Cabrita Mateus, *A PIDE/DGS na Guerra Colonial 1961–1974* [The PIDE/DGS in the Colonial War 1961–1974] (Lisbon: Terramar, 2004), pp. 199–207.
40 Pires Nunes, *Angola 1966–74,* p. 19.
41 Pires Nunes, *Siroco*, p. 25.
42 Pires Nunes, *Angola 1966–74,* p. 42.
43 Carlos Acabado, *Kinda e outras histórias de uma guerra esquecida* [Kinda and Other Stories of a Forgotten War] (Linda-a-Velha: DG Edições, 2011), p. 9.
44 José Augusto Queiroga, "Histórias Vividas: Por Terras do Fim do Mundo,

Uma viagem entre os 18 e os 9 graus de Latitude Sul" [Tales Lived: For the Lands at the End of the Earth, A trip between 18 and 9 degrees South Latitude], p. 6, undated deposition, Caixa 181, Archivo Histórico de Força Aérea, Alfragide.
45 Acabado, *Kinda*, p. 51.
46 Comissão para o Estudo das Campanhas de África, *Resenha Histórico-Militar das Campanhas de África 1961–1974, 6 Volume, Tomo I, Angola–Livro 2*, p. 356.
47 Acabado, *Kinda*, pp. 136–137.
48 Ibid., p. 6.
49 Mário Diniz and Luís Proença, "AL III, História Breve de uma Vida Longa, 1963–2013" [AL III, Brief History of a Long Life], *Mais Alto* 404 (July–August 2013): p. 24.

Chapter 3

1 António Ferrand d'Almeida, "Cavalaria a Cavalao em Angola?" [Horse Cavalry in Angola?], *Revista da Cavalaria* (1963 annual issue): pp. 289–292.
2 José Talhadas, *Memórias de um guerreiro colonial* [Memories of a Colonial Warrior] (Lisbon: Ancora, 2010) p. 48.
3 Ibid., pp. 37–38.
4 António Ferrand d'Almeida, "Emprego da cavalaria a cavalo em Angola: Sim" [Using Horse Cavalry in Angola: Yes], *Revista da Cavalaria* (1964 annual issue): pp. 231–243.
5 Luís Barros e Cunha, "A cavalaria a cavalo no ultramar: meios e missões" [Horse Cavalry in the *ultramar*: Means and Missions], *Revista da Cavalaria* (1965 annual issue): pp. 269–281.
6 U.S. Marine Corps, *Small Wars Manual* (Washington: Government Printing Office, 1940), pp. 3/25–35.
7 António Ferrand d'Almeida, "Recordações de um 'Dragão de Angola'" [Recollections of a "Dragoon of Angola"], *Revista Militar* (October–November 1985): p. 695.
8 Adriano Victor Hugo Landerset Cadima, Office of the Chief of Staff of the Army, "Memorandum for the record: Horse Units for the Military Region of Angola," 1 February 1968, Archivo Histórico Militar.
9 Peter Abbott and Manuel Ribeiro Rodrigues, *Modern African Wars (2): Angola and Mozambique 1961–1974* (London: Osprey, 1988), p. 24.
10 Luís Manuel Silveira Vicente da Silva, "Uma Cavalaria em Agonia? [A Cavalry in Agony?], *Revista da Cavalaria* (1971 annual issue): pp. 174–181.
11 Landerset Cadima, "Memorandum for the record: Horse Units for the Military Region of Angola."
12 Ibid.
13 Miguel Freire, "Dragoons of Angola," *Osprey Military Journal* 4, issue 4: p. 47.
14 Landerset Cadima, "Memorandum for the record: Horse Units for the Military Region of Angola."
15 Ferrand d'Almeida, "Recordações de um 'Dragão de Angola'," p. 699.
16 Miguel Freire, "Dragões de Angola: Fighting Insurgency from Horseback," *Armor* (May–June 1998): p. 36.
17 Miguel Freire, "Dragoons of Angola," *Osprey Military Journal* 4, issue 4: p. 49.
18 Ferrand d'Almeida, "Recordoções de um 'Dragão de Angola'," p. 704.
19 José Luís Núncio Fragoso, "Contribuição para o estudo do emprgo das tropas a cavalo em Angola – relatório de final de comissão (Abril de 1970 – Abril de 1972)" [Contribution to the study of the employment of horse troops in Angola – final report of the commission (April 1970 – April 1972)] (Luanda: Região Militar de Angola, 1972), pp. 3–7.
20 Ibid., pp. 704–705.
21 Miguel Freire, "Dragoons of Angola," *Osprey Military Journal* 4, No. 4: p. 49.
22 Núncio Fragoso, "Contribuição para o estudo do emprgo das tropas a cavalo em Angola – relatório de final de comissão (Abril de 1970 – Abril de 1972)," p. 10.
23 Ibid.
24 Ferrand d'Almeida, "Recordoções de um 'Dragão de Angola'," p. 705.
25 Luís Barros e Cunha, "A cavalaria a cavalo no ultramar: algumas reflexões" [Horse Cavalry in the *ultramar*: Some reactions], *Revista da Cavalaria* (1967 annual issue): p. 277.
26 J.A. (initials only), "Cavalaria a cavalo em Angola" [Horse cavalry in Angola], *Revista da Cavalaria* (1969 annual issue): p. 171.
27 Ferrand d'Almeida, "Recordoções de um 'Dragão de Angola'," p. 705.
28 Academia Militar, "Instrucão de Tactica de Cavalaria – O Pelotão a Cavalo" [Tactical Instruction of Cavalry – The Horse Platoon] (Lisbon: Academia Militar, 1943, as revised), p. 1.
29 Luís Manuel Silveira Vicente da Silva, "Lances de «Calvao» no «Xadrez» Angolano" [Moves of the "knight" on the Angolan "chessboard"], *Jornal do Exército* (June 1972): p. 28.
30 Academia Militar, "Instrucão de Tactica de Cavalaria – O Pelotão a Cavalo", p. 1.
31 Ferrand d'Almeida, "Recordoções de um 'Dragão de Angola'," p. 695–705.
32 Ibid., p. 705.
33 Núncio Fragoso, "Contribuição para o estudo do emprgo das tropas a cavalo em Angola – relatório de final de comissão (Abril de 1970 – Abril de 1972)," p. 10.
34 Ferrand d'Almeida, "Recordoções de um 'Dragão de Angola'," p. 693.
35 Ibid., p. 709.
36 Ibid.
37 Colonel César Augusto Rodrigues Mano, interview by the author, 10 November 1994, Oeiras, Portugal. Colonel Mano commanded Cavalry Group No. 1 (*Grupo de Cavalaria No. 1*) in Silva Porto, Angola, between 1973 and 1974.
38 Ferrand d'Almeida, "Recordoções de um 'Dragão de Angola'," p. 693.
39 Ibid., p. 710.
40 Miguel Freire, interview by the author, 6 April 2018, Carcavellos, Portugal.
41 Mano interview, 10 November 1994.
42 Ferrand d'Almeida, "Recordações de um 'Dragão de Angola'," p. 710.
43 Ibid., p. 711.
44 Ibid., p. 712.
45 Francisco Aragão, *Tropas Negras* [Black Troops] (Lisbon: Seara Nova, 1926), p. 68.
46 Ibid., p. 693.
47 Miguel Freire, "Dragões de Angola," p. 38 and pp. 48–49.
48 Ferrand d'Almeida, "Recordações de um 'Dragão de Angola'," p. 712–713.
49 Ibid.
50 Ibid.
51 Ibid., p. 49.
52 Mano interview, 10 November 1994.
53 Academia Militar, "Instrucão de Tactica de Cavalaria – O Pelotão a Cavalo", pp. 1–4.
54 Academia Militar, "Instrucão de Tactica de Cavalaria – O Pelotão a Cavalo", p. 5–8.
55 Miguel Freire, "Dragões de Angola," p. 47.
56 Mano interview, 10 November 1994.
57 Henrique Matteus, "A Acção da Cavalaria no Leste de Angola" [Cavalry Action in the East of Angola], *Revista da Cavalaria* (March 2009): pp. 17–18.
58 Abbott and Ribeiro Rodrigues, *Modern African Wars (2)*, p. 24.
59 Ferrand d'Almeida, "Recordações de um 'Dragão de Angola'," p. 698.
60 Barros e Cunha, "A cavalaria a cavalo no ultramar: meios e missões," p. 277.
61 Miguel Freire, "Dragoons of Angola," *Osprey Military Journal* 4, issue 4: p. 47.
62 Ibid.
63 Miguel Freire, "Back on Horseback! Finding adaptive tactics for counterinsurgency in 1960s and 1970s," paper delivered at the XLI Congress of the International Commission of Military History (ICMH), Beijing, China, on 1 September 2015, p. 15.
64 Miguel Freire, "Dragoons of Angola," p. 47.
65 Ibid.
66 Landerset Cadima, "Memorandum for the record: Horse Units for the Military Region of Angola."
67 Ibid.
68 Ibid.
69 Memorandum from Vice Chief of the Army Staff, Horácio José de Sá Viana Rebelo, to the Secretariat General of National Defence, 13 February 1968, Aquivo Histórico Militar
70 Joaquim M. Mensurado, *Os Páras na Guerra, 1961–63 and 1968–72* [Paras at War, 1961–63 and 1968–72] (Lisbon: Prefácio, 2002), pp. 54–55.
71 Ibid., p. 55.
72 Ibid., p. 56.
73 António Ferrand d'Almeida, "A Cavalaria a Cavalo" [Horse Cavalry] in *Resenha Histórico-Militar das Campanhas de África 1961–1974* [Military History Review of the African Campaigns 1961–1974], Volume 6 (Aspects of Operational Activity), Tome 1, Angola–Book 2 by the Commission for the Study of the African Campaigns (Lisbon: Estado-Maior do Exército, 2006), pp. 320–327.
74 Miguel Freire, "Dragoons of Angola," p. 49.
75 Ferrand d'Almeida, "A Cavalaria a Cavalo", p. 326.
76 Henrique Mateus, "A acção da cavalaria no Leste de Angola" [Cavalry Action in the East of Angola], *Revista da Cavalaria* (March 2009): pp. 17–18.
77 Ferrand d'Almeida, "A Cavalaria a Cavalo", p. 326.
78 Ibid., pp. 326–327.
79 Ibid., p. 327.
80 Carlos Acabado, *Kinda e outras histórias de uma guerra esquecida* [Kinda and Other Stories of a Forgotten War] (Linda-a-Velha: DG Edições, 2011), pp. 154–155.
81 Hélio Felgas, "Opinião" [Opinion], as quoted in *Resenha Histórico-Militar das Campanhas de África, 1961–1974*, 6th Volume, Tome I, Book 2, p. 450.
82 Daniel Chipenda, "Revolta do Leste" [Revolt of the East] in *A Guerra de África, 1961–1974* [The War of Africa, 1961–1974], by José Freire Antunes (Lisbon: Temas e Debates, 1996), p. 851.
83 António Silva Cardoso, *Angola, Anatomia de uma Tragédia* [Angola, Anatomy of a Tragedy] (Lisbon: Oficina do Livro, 2000), p. 302.
84 Ibid., p. 292.

Chapter 4

1 John A. Marcum, *The Angolan Revolution: Volume I, The Anatomy of an Explosion (1950–1962)* (Cambridge: MIT Press, 1969), p. 234.
2 António de Jesus Bispo, "A Participação da Força Aérea na Guerra de África (1961–1975)" [Air Force Participation in the African War (1961–1975)], *Revista Militar* 2507 (December 2010): p. 1396.
3 Ibid.
4 António José Telo, *História da Marinha Portuguesa: Homens, Doutrinas e*

Organização, 1824-1974 (Tomo I) [History of the Portuguese Navy: Men, Doctrine and Organization, 1824–1974 (Volume I)] (Lisbon: Academia de Marinha, 1999), p. 616.
5 Adelino Serras Pires and Fiona Claire Capstick, *The Winds of Havoc* (New York: St. Martin's Press, 2001), p. 83.
6 Al J. Venter, *The Zambesi Salient* (Cape Town: Howard Timmins, 1974), pp. 47–48.
7 Telo, *História da Marinha Portuguesa,* p. 616.
8 Henrik Ellert, *The Rhodesian Front War, Counter-insurgency and Guerrilla Warfare 1962–1980* (Gweru, Zimbabwe: Mambo Press, 1993), p. 88.
9 Neil Bruce, "Portugal's African Wars," *Conflict Studies*, No. 34 (March 1973): p. 22.
10 Aniceto Afonso and Carlos de Matos Gomes, *Guerra Colonial* [Colonial War] (Lisbon, Notícias, 2001), pp. 168–173.
11 Comissão para o Estudo das Campanhas de África (1961–1974), *Resenha Histórico-Militar das Campanhas de África (1961–1974), 14º Volume, Comandos, Tomo 1, Grupos Iniciais* [Historical-Military Report on the African Campaigns (1961–1974), 14th Volume, Commandos, Book 1, Initial Groups] (Lisbon: Estado-Maior do Exército, 2009), p. 569.
12 Comissão para o Estudo das Campanhas de África (1961–1974), *Resenha Histórico-Militar das Campanhas de África (1961–1974), 6º Volume, Aspectos da Actividade Operacional, Tomo 1II, Moçambique, Livro I* [Historical-Military Report on the African Campaigns (1961–1974), 6th Volume, Aspects of Operational Activity, Tome III, Mozambique, Book I] (Lisbon: Estado-Maior do Exército, 2012), pp. 723–730.
13 Jorge Mathias, *Tropas a Cavalo: Subsídios para o estudo do seu emprego em Moçambique* [Cavalry Troops: Aids for the study of their use in Mozambique] (Nampula: Região Militar de Moçambique, 1970).
14 Ibid., pp. 11–12.
15 Carlos Manuel Dias de Almeida, "O Esquadrão a Cavalao de Moçambique ne Guerra do Ultramar" [The Cavalry Squadron of Mozambique in theWar of the Ultramar], *Revista da Cavalaria* (March 2009): p. 22.
16 Carlos Manuel Dias de Almeida, *História da Unidade – 1° Esquadrão a Cavalo/ RMM* [Unit History – 1st Suuadron of Cavalry/RMM] (Lisbon: Estado Maior do Exército, 1981), p. 21.
17 Ibid., p. 22.
18 Ibid.
19 Miguel Freire, "Back on Horseback! Finding adaptive tactics for counterinsurgency in 1960s and 1970s," paper delivered at the XLI Congress of the International Commission of Military History (ICMH), Beijing, China, on 1 September 2015, p. 19.
20 Dias de Almeida, *História da Unidade,* p. 55.
21 Ibid., p. 53.
22 Ibid., p. 54.
23 Ibid., p. 22.
24 Ibid., p. 47.
25 Ibid.
26 Ibid.
27 Ibid.
28 Ibid.
29 Ibid.
30 Ibid.
31 Ibid., pp. 47–48.
32 Ibid.
33 Ibid., pp. 5–6.
34 Ibid., p. 59.
35 Ibid., pp 60–61.
36 Miguel Freire, "Back on Horseback! ", p. 19.
37 Dias de Almeida, *História da Unidade,* p. 59.
38 Ibid., p. 65.
39 Ibid., p. 66.
40 Ibid., p. 67.
41 Ibid., pp. 66–67.
42 Ibid., p. 68.
43 Ibid., p. 65.
44 Ibid., p. 67.
45 Ibid., pp. 62–65.

Chapter 5

1 António Ferrand d'Almeida, "Recordações de um 'Dragão de Angola'" [Recollections of a "Dragoon of Angola"], *Revista Militar* (October–November 1985): pp. 715–717.
2 Patrick Ollivier, *Commandos de Brousse* [Bush Commandos] (Paris: Bernard Grasset, 1985); and Alexandre Binda, *The Equus Men, Rhodesia's Mounted Infantry: The Grey's Scouts 1896–1980* (Solihull, UK: Helion and Co., 2015).
3 Willem Steenkamp, *South Africa's Border War 1966-1989* (Gibraltar: Ashanti Publishing Limited, 1989), p. 201.
4 Willem S. van der Waals, *Portugal's War in Angola 1961–1974* (Rivonia: Ashanti Publishing, 1993), p. 196.